CANE RO[D]
TIPS & TAPERS

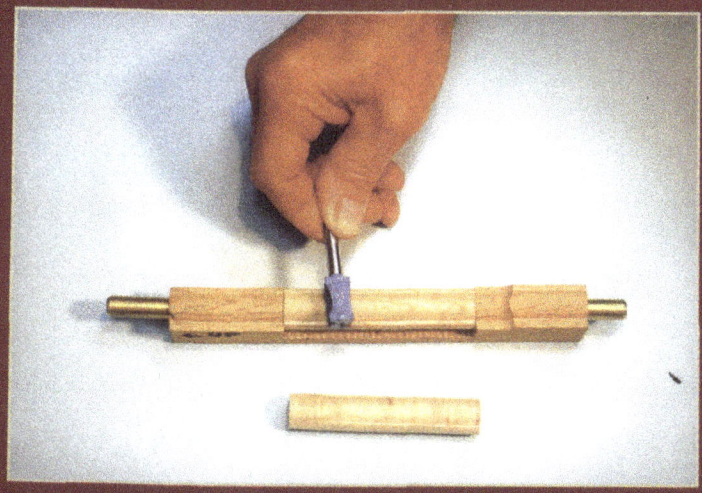

RAY GOULD

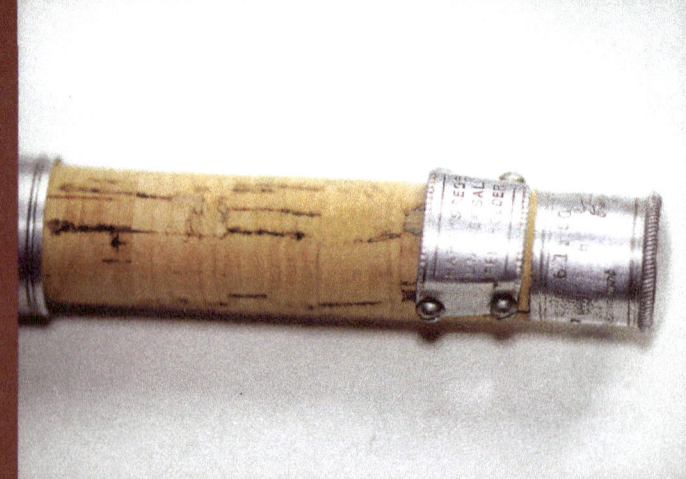

CANE RODS
TIPS & TAPERS

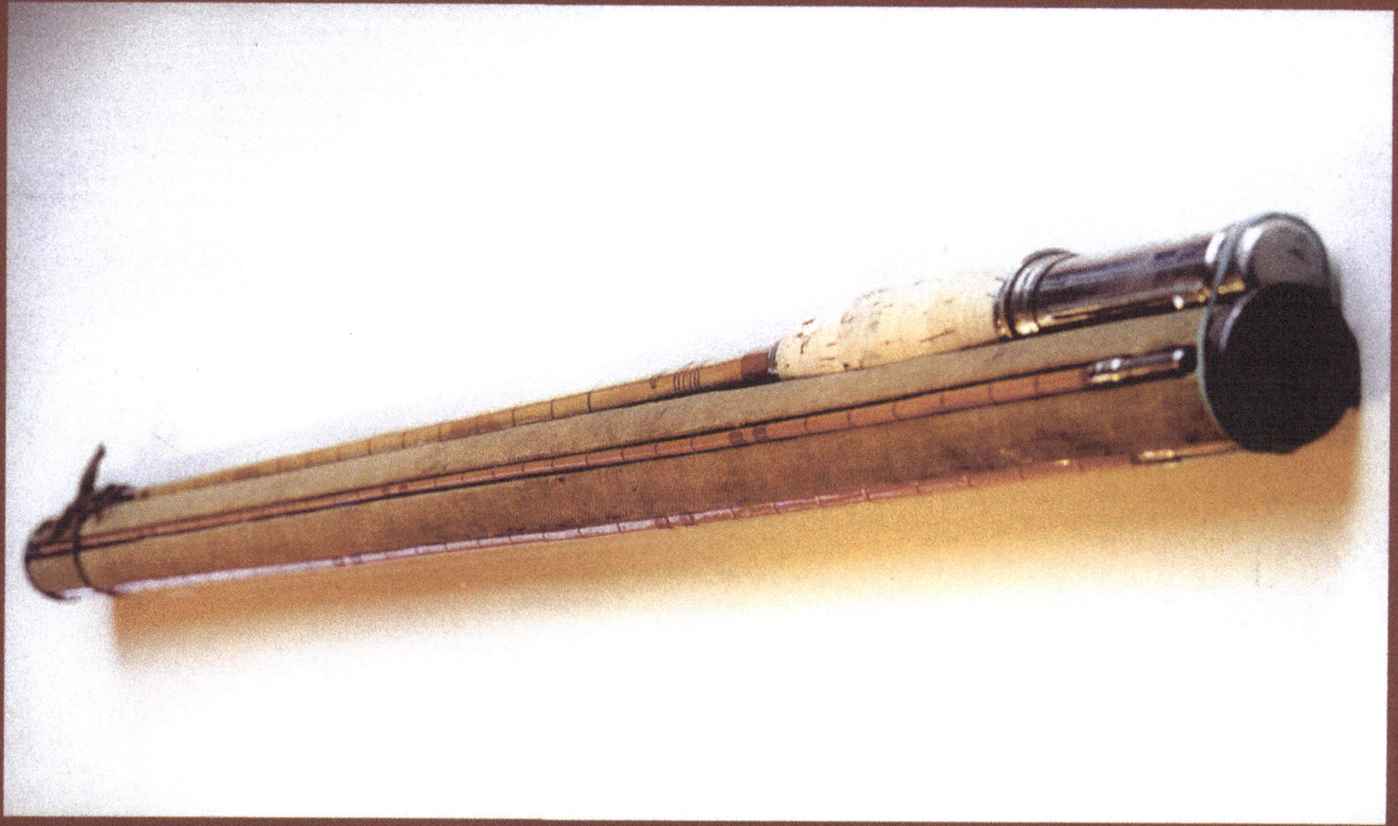

RAY GOULD

E P B M
ECHO POINT BOOKS & MEDIA, LLC

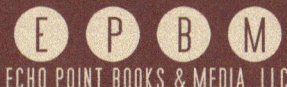

Dedication

This book is dedicated to my wonderful thirteen-year-old granddaughter Kirsten Kathleen Gould whose bright spirit and enthusiasm touched everyone who knew her or who read some of her writings. Grandpa enjoyed introducing her to fly-fishing for those fantastic Kamloops trout in the wilds of British Columbia, and her Dad took her fishing for coho salmon whereby she out-fished everyone.

Kirsten was an exceptional student and the kind of person one dreams about having for a granddaughter. She was raised and loved deeply by a wonderful family including her mother Dawn, father Kevin, brother Steven, and sister Lauren. She was also supported by her grandparents as well as many, many school friends and extraordinary neighbors. Kirsten was honored by the "Make a Wish" Foundation allowing her to take twenty of her closest young friends on a very nice local boat cruise while enjoying music from a band, and then Kirsten and her closest friend spent a night at a fancy hotel in Seattle. That wish exemplifies the kind of person she was.

Kirsten succumbed at the age of thirteen to the effects of Ewings Sarcoma, a rare children's cancer, after having received every possible type of treatment at Children's Hospital in Seattle. We miss her very much.

Acknowledgements

The photographic skills of Joe Poehlman deserve special mention. His ability to produce clear imagery in an eye-catching way is unusual and adds a great deal to the final product of this book.

The continued enthusiasm and creativeness of my friend and rod-building cohort Jack Byrd serves as inspiration to me in continuing my work on cane rods. His focus on upgrading tools and equipment to do their jobs better and simpler demonstrates what is possible if one puts his mind to it.

Another whole dimension to the design of rod-making equipment has been shown by Theron Chamberlain, a long-time fly fishing partner and friend. He has used his expertise in tool making, design, and engineering skills to invent equipment that takes the drudgery from rod making. His designs are unique and yet demonstrate the simplicity that is the hallmark of well-engineered machinery.

I'm indebted to Eric Meyerson for the outstanding photograph of cane rods built by the old masters and the excellent story accompanying it. Eric is an exceptionally fine caster and one who understands the workmanship, history and detail of a fine bamboo fly rod.

To the avid fly fishermen who join me at Glimpse Lake each year to chase the wily Kamloops trout and to field test my latest cane rod designs, I give special thanks. I salute Bob Barr, Bill Booth, Jack Byrd, Theron Chamberlain, Hugh Clark, Earl Gutschmidt, Dick Hankinson, Russ Hardy, Tom Hodgson, Bruce Johnson, Bill Johnston, Bob Lindemeyer, John Narver, Maury Skeith, Wilbur Watson and Marv Young.

A World of Hope
By Kirsten Gould

I hold in my hand
A world of hope,
A world of peace,
A world to cope.

In this world are many treasures,
Happiness, joy and lots of pleasures.

You'll never hear a discouraging word,
Only compliments will be heard.

Disease is foreign in this place,
Unhappy frowns aren't seen on any face.

Summer and flowers are always in bloom,
There's never a single cloud of gloom.

Follow the rainbow and you will find,
This life full of wonders of every kind.

I hold in my hand
A world of hope,
A world of peace,
A world to cope.

Published by Echo Point Books & Media
Brattleboro, Vermont
www.EchoPointBooks.com

All rights reserved.
Neither this work nor any portions thereof may be reproduced, stored in a retrieval system, or transmitted in any capacity without written permission from the publisher.

Copyright © 2005, 2016 by Ray Gould

Cane Rods: Tips and Tapers
ISBN: 978-1-62654-551-9 (paperback)

Interior design by Jerry Hutchinson

Cover design by Rachel Gualco
Echo Point Books & Media

Table Of Contents

Introduction 6

Tip No. 1 - *Maximizing Rod Performance* 7

Tip No. 2 - *Heat treating and Moisture Control* 9

Tip No. 3 - *Color Toning* 11

Tip No. 4 - *Byrd's Machine Planing device* 12

Tip No. 5 - *Chamberlain Spline Milling Mechanism* 16

Tip No. 6 - *The Tensioner* 21

Tip No. 7 - *Ferrules* 22

Tip No. 8 - *Guide Spacing* 25

Tip No. 9 - *Grips* 26

Tip No. 10 - *Rod Wrapping* 28

Tip No. 11 - *Maker's label* 30

Tip No. 12 - *Finishing and Gluing* 32

Tip No. 13 - *Nodeless Rods* 34

Tip No. 14 - *Quadrate Rods and Tapers* 36

Tip No. 15 - *Spiral Rod Making* 40

Tip No. 16 - *Short Rod Tapers for Rods 4'4" to 6' 10"* 42

Tip No. 17 - *Spey Rod Tapers* 45

Tip No. 18 - *Spinning Rod and Casting Rod Tapers* 47

Tip No. 19 - *Pentagonal Rods* 49

Tip No. 20 - *Taper Collection* 51

Tip No. 21 - *Understanding Rod Actions* 88

Tip No. 22 - *Where to Find It* 93

Introduction

This book is intended as an aid to those who wish to pursue the art of cane-rod making or repairing. The reader will find a wealth of information regarding those methods, devices and techniques that can only be learned by testing, trial and error. Many "tips" are described to guide the rod-maker in how to accomplish a particular and unusually difficult task. While a number of books and references are available for the basics of rod-building, this book focuses on specific information and problem solving.

Of special interest is an often sought after collection of nearly 300 rod tapers by many famous rod-builders. Using this information a rod-builder can duplicate the action and design of an "old master," or try a favorite tried-and-true model. In addition, when a replacement rod section is required, the dimensional data for many models is listed.

Ed Hartzell planing cane.

TIP NO. 1
Maximizing Rod Performance

FINDING THE SPINE

There are some important steps that may be taken prior to the final assembly of a cane rod to enhance the way it casts. Like most fishing rods, ones made of bamboo have a "spine" or stiffest plane in which to load the rod. In the case of hexagonal cane rods, this is most likely caused by variations in the physical properties and dimensions of each of the six (6) strips constituting that particular rod. The reason this is important is that the guides should be located on the "soft" side to allow maximum power to be generated during casting, and so that the rod will oscillate and dampen in a single plane.

There are two ways to find the "spine". This must be done after the rod sections are glued up, cleaned off and straightened but before the guides, wraps, reel seat, cork grip and varnish are applied. The rationale for this sequence is that the installation of the guides will somewhat change the stiffness of the plane on which they are placed. One method for determining the "spine" is to position a rod section at a 45-degree angle to a flat surface with one end resting on that surface and the other end cradled loosely in one hand. With the other hand, gently deflect the section at its midpoint and roll the section back and forth. See Fig. 2.

A noticeable "kick" will be observed wherein the rod section prefers to stay in a certain position. Mark the flat that is down (on the outside of the curved rod section) since this is the "soft" side. This is the flat upon which the guides are to be

Finding the spine. Method 1.

Finding the spine. Method 2.

mounted. Note too that this means that the flat opposite of the "soft" side must be the "strong" side. Thus when the rod is loaded, ready to present the forward power cast, the strong side will deliver maximum power to the line.

Another method for finding the "spine" is to position the rod section vertically with one end (the smaller-diameter end) resting on a flat surface. Then with a finger pressing straight down on the upper end of that section, notice that the rod section will bend and "kick" to one side. See Fig. 2. Mark the flat that is on the outside of the curved rod section. This will again be the "soft" flat and the one upon which the guides are to be mounted.

Once again, what takes place when the guides are mounted in this way is that the strongest spine is loaded in tension when the line is picked up off the water during the first part of a cast and then has energy stored in it while under compression during the last half of the back cast as the rod is brought forward to deliver the fly.

SYNCHRONIZING

When all the sections of a rod are assembled after having found the "spine" of each individual section and locating its guides accordingly, a rod is said to be "synchronized". It means that all the rod sections will work together in the same way to deliver the fly and it will oscillate and dampen vibrations in the same plane.

BALANCING

A further step in obtaining the maximum performance from a rod is to construct it in such a way that it is "balanced". This is a process by which a single-handed rod is made comfortable for the caster and requires a minimum of effort or strength to use. The factors involved include: The position of the reel, the weight of the reel and line, the type of reel seat, the length of the cork grip, the center line of the cork grip, the

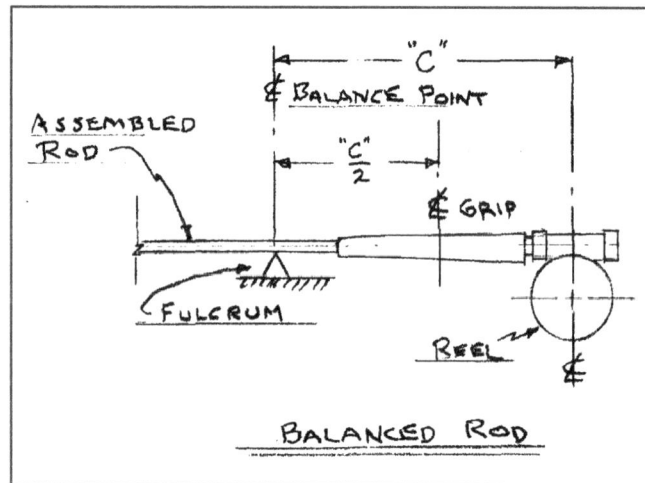

Fig. 4: Finding the balance point.

weight of the ferrules, the length of the rod, and the center of balance. To determine the center of balance, assemble the rod including the reel to be used. Position the rod horizontally and balance it on a fulcrum. See Fig. 4.

The balance point should be such that the centerline of the cork grip (half of its length) is half way (dimension "C/2") between the balance point (dimension "C") and the centerline of the reel. The grip should be long enough to allow the hand to be moved along the length of the cork to find a comfortable position where the rod does not feel tip heavy nor butt heavy. A sliding band reel seat allows some adjustment in the location of the reel to help obtain a suitable balance. It is also noteworthy that an up-locking reel seat tends to position the reel farther toward the rod tip whereas a down-locking reel seat moves the reel seat towards the butt. Additional adjustment can be obtained by using a heavier or lighter reel. (Note: this system may not be practical for rods with very short cork grips in which case the balance point should be close to the front end of the grip).

Tip No. 2
Heat Treatment and Moisture Control

Preventing Culm Cracking While Aging
One easy-to-perform step in the aging and storage of culms prior to their use is to coat the ends of the culm with wax mixed with paint thinner. This will reduce the extent of random cracks along the culm and is effective because most of the moisture in the cane is lost through the end grain. Water travels along the length of the culm through tubules in nature's pathway and is one of least resistance.

How to Heat Treat
There are some that believe the best way to heat-treat the bamboo is to first warm it up to a temperature of about 200°F. and hold it there for a couple of hours. This gently drives out the moisture before raising the temperature to 350°F. as is done in the final heat-treating. The reasoning behind this procedure is that it prevents rupturing the cells in the cane. Note too that the natural moisture content of bamboo is about 12-13%, whereas during heat-treating it can be driven down close to zero and then will return to about 5-6% after about 20 days (while stored inside).

There are a number of systems used to apply the heat used in heat-treating the cane. One method is called "flaming" where a propane torch or a blowtorch is used to heat the outside of the culm to a rich brown shade. Care must be taken in this process not to burn the bamboo too deeply causing it to lose its physical properties. Another similar system is known as the "ring of fire" where the culm is passed through the center of a gas-fired circular section of pipe equipped with orifices directing the flame inward.

Another common method is to devise a horizontally mounted oven heated by a strip heater or by a vertical oven heated by a hot air gun. Most all of these are temperature controlled via thermostat or use circulated air and a thermometer. Most commonly, the heat-treat temperature is in the 325- to 375-degree-Fahrenheit range.

The Effects of Heat Treating
Various rod-builders have run tests to determine the effects of heat-treating bamboo. The results vary widely and leave the rod-builder perplexed and wondering just exactly what to do in this regard. Claude Kreider described in his book, *The Bamboo Fly Rod and How to Build It*, published in 1951, a heat-treatment method using a steel pipe heated by a blowtorch and the application of ammonia carbonate crystal (see Fig. 5).

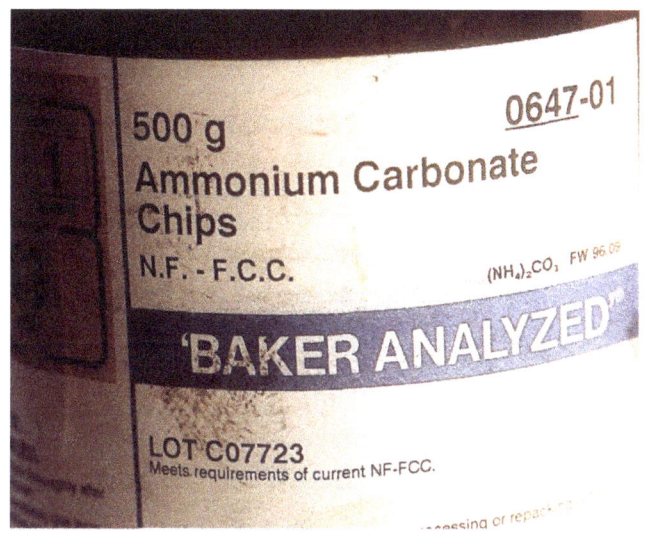
Ammonia carbonate bottle label.

The procedure used was to heat the pipe until it just ceases exhausting steam vapors and the color of the cane reached the desired tone. He also reported that Lew Stoner of the Winston Co. believed that heat-treating increased the rod's stiffness and power by as much as 25%.

George Barnes states in his book *How to Make Bamboo Fly Rods* published in 1977, that the purpose of heat-treating is to harden and strengthen the cane and that untreated bamboo tends to plane and shape easier than that which has been heat-treated.

In Garrison's book *A Master's Guide to Building a Bamboo Fly Rod* published in 1977, it is stated that heat-treating under pressure drives off the excess moisture and resins that tend to keep the cane soft, and that when the binding pressure is released the strips show increased strength and stiffness and should be very straight. Furthermore, he concluded that all six strips to be used in a rod section should be bound together and heat-treated at the same time, and that the tight binding prevented the nodes from re-kinking during this treatment. His procedure was to cook the butt strips longer than the tip strips to be certain that the heat can penetrate to the inner fibers. He also varied the time in the heat-treating oven with the size of the rod wherein larger rods were cooked longer. His preferred temperature was 350°F with a time of 5 1/4 to 8 1/2 minutes.

The Orvis Company, in research published titled "Comparison of Bamboo, Graphite and Glass Rods", found that untempered bamboo "softens" (reduction in flexural strength) by 7.5% after 27,000 double flexes, whereas tempered bamboo softened only by 4.6%.

In 1990, Don Anderson, (Alberta, Canada), an excellent rod-builder and a fine caster, published the results of his tempering tests. He prepared strips all from the same culm as follows:

Method 1 = flamed
Method 2 = 360°F for 6 minutes
Method 3 = Raw cane not tempered
Method 4 = 300°F for 10 minutes
Method 5 = 250°F for 30 minutes
Method 6 = 400°F for 6 minutes

These strips were then subjected to three tests: deflection, oscillation and set (permanent deformation) with the following overall results (lowest rating number is best). It was noted that the deflection test and the "set" test were best for both the flamed strip and the 250°F strip, while the oscillation test was the same for all strips.

Preparation Method	Rating (lowest number is best)
Flamed	2.085
360°F for 6 minutes	5.42
Raw cane	3.41
300°F for 10 minutes	4.25
250°F for 30 minutes	2.25
400°F for 6 minutes	3.5

Don also reported that the flamed strips, the 360°F strips, the raw cane strips and the 300°F strips all planed smoothly with even shavings.

In 1992, Wayne Cattanach, in his book *Handcrafting Bamboo Fly Rods* recommends that heat-treating should be done at 375°F for seven (7) minutes, then flipped end for end and baked an additional 3 1/2 minutes. He points out that the effect is to relax the internodal sweeps, drive out the moisture and temper it.

In 1995 tests conducted by well-known rod-builder Tom Fulk of Anacortes, Washington, various sets of three strips were heated to 275°F, 300°F, 325°F, 350°F and 375°F. The strips were then subjected to deflection tests anticipating that a correlation might occur between the heat exposure and the resistance to bending. However none occurred.

In 2001, Bob Nunley reported that after testing strips at various temperatures and times, the ones that were stronger in both directions than others tested were blond strips and flamed strips heat treated at 375°F for 12 minutes.

R.E. Milward suggests in his book *Fact, Fiction and Flyrods* published in 2001 that the combination of bamboo characteristics and requirements is the reason why it must be heat treated at a temperature high enough to cause some color change.

He concludes that drying bamboo causes a "huge" and permanent gain in bending strength, yet any darkening of the color represents loss of tensile and flexural strength. He further argues that flaming and oven-brown toning are not recommended.

My own recommendations on heat-treating based on experience, data collection and testing fall into five categories:

1. Straightness

There is no question but that a major advantage of heat-treating is that the individual splines become much straighter after they are unbound from heat-treating. This makes it much easier for the rod-builder to finish the strips to final dimension.

2. Planing

I personally like the way heat-treated splines plane. The plane blade seems to dig in much less at the nodes.

3. Strength

There are many indications that bamboo does indeed gain in strength after heat-treating. The trick is to heat treat the cane at the right temperature and for the right period of time. Heat-treating tightly-bound splines at 350°F for eleven (11) minutes in the presence of ammonia carbonate crystals continues to work best for me, and is close to the parameters used by many rod-builders. Using this system the cane will still be blond to straw colored and it will not degrade the properties of the fibers.

4. Weight and Stability

Tests by Tom Morgan of the Winston Company and Jess Wells of Portland, Oregon both verify that bamboo culms as delivered have a moisture content of 11-13%. Heat treatment drives the moisture content down close to zero but then it returns to about 5% after some 20 days or so. The result is a reduction in weight due to the loss of volatiles and moisture but produces a stable material with enough moisture to provide good adhesion for gluing. My own tests have shown that the size of an individual strip in thickness (from the point of the apex to the enamel on a hex rod strip) is reduced by 0.003" during heat-treating. This is one of the reasons to heat-treat before bringing the splines to final dimension.

5. Aesthetics and Coloration

My preference is to produce straw-colored rods, yet many other builders prefer making rods with a mottled or flamed appearance. This indeed can produce handsome rods and is best done with a torch of some type. It takes practice to get the cane dark enough to be pleasing yet not burned to the point of ruining the mechanical properties of the fiber. Bear in mind that much of the dark color is lost when the enamel is removed during the final steps in bringing the splines to size. When all the factors are considered, it is most certainly best to heat-treat bamboo.

TIP NO. 3
Color Toning

Color toning is a process by which bamboo is darkened to a brown tone by exposing it to ammonia gas while inside a closed container. **Be advised that this procedure is dangerous since the ammonia gas fumes are noxious. Great care and ventilation is required. Do this job outdoors or in a detached shop or garage.** Note too that the difference between this and staining wood is that the cane is not placed in direct contact with a liquid thus there is no streaking nor runs in the color.

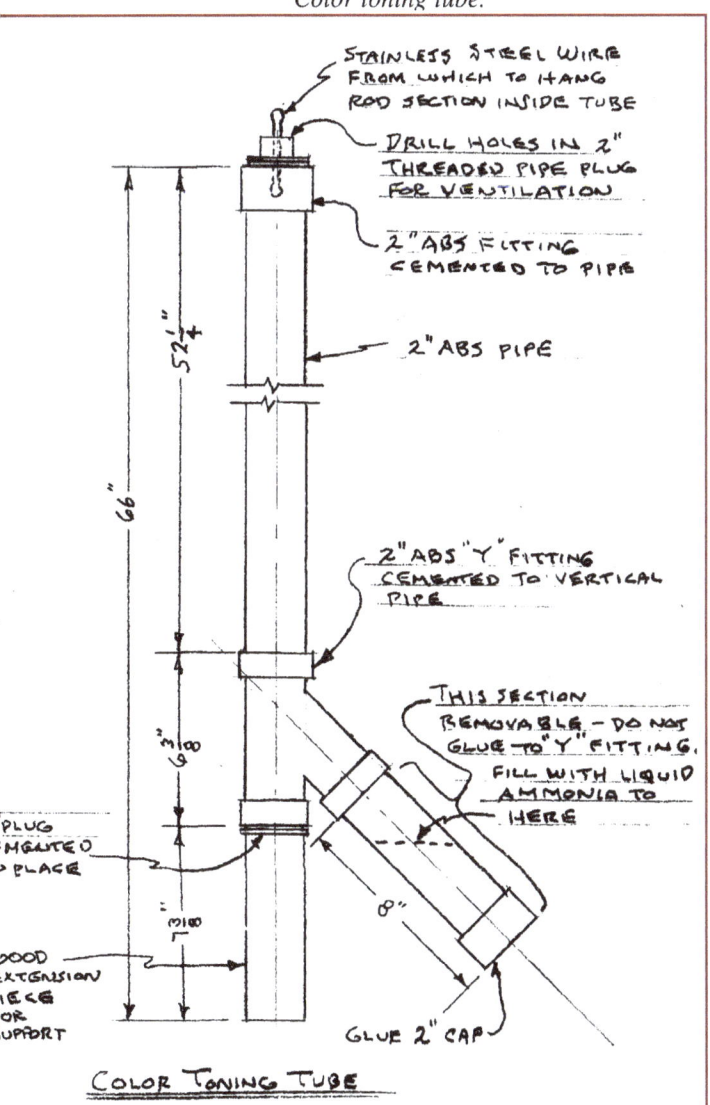

Color toning tube.

To perform color toning effectively the use of a strong solution of ammonia is required. Twenty-six percent (26%) ammonia hydoxide is available from some engineering drafting supply houses in one (1)-gallon bottles. This agent may be placed in the offshoot leg of a plastic pipe container designed to use for this application. This color-toning tube is shown in the photo Fig.6. It is constructed of 2" ABS plastic piping and cemented together. The wood tube on the bottom is simply a support leg so that the tube will stand more easily upright.

Note that the top cap is threaded so as to be removable and has been drilled for ventilation purposes and also to incorporate a stainless-steel wire on which to hang the rod sections inside the tube. The forty-five (45)-degree leg piece has a sliding fit (not cemented) to the main vertical tube so that it may be removed and filled with the ammonia liquid. Hang the rod after it is glued up but before it is finished in the color-toning tube. Check the color of the cane after each twenty-four (24)-hour period to determine if the desired tone has been attained. The effectiveness and speed with which the ammonia reacts is enhanced by temperature. Thus, performing the toning on a warm day or warming the ammonia will require less time. It is wise to practice by color toning a short sample rod section before moving on to the rod itself, and then applying varnish to that test piece to see the final result.

Heat-treating in the presence of ammonia carbonate crystals also is a system to color-tone a rod. The cane turns straw colored or slightly brown through this procedure depending somewhat on the time and temperatures used. This process is described in the chapter on heat-treating.

Several other ways of darkening the cane have been used with success and are less hazardous than using ammonia. Waterproof marking pens (the Pantone type is popular), stain sticks, leather dye and wood tints have been used by some rod-builders with good results. A particularly easy way to attain brown toning is by using Lincoln Light Brown leather dye. Apply it evenly to the glued-up blank that is already fitted with ferrules, cork grip, tip top and reel seat, but before any wrappings are applied. Wiping the dye on with a clean cloth seems to work best. Let dry thoroughly after the right tone is attained, then varnish the blank before any other work is done.

Tip No. 4
Byrd's Machine Planing Device

The information in this chapter describes in detail a unique device for producing tapered splines as created by Jack Byrd of Edmonds, Washington. Jack is well known in the Northwest as a rod-builder and has co-chaired one of the rod-building workshops held biennially at the Corbett Lake Country Inn in British Columbia, Canada. He is also a long-time member and former officer of the Olympic Fly Fishers club. What is important and unusual about this machine is its simplicity and relatively low cost. It can be made in the average home workshop to help the rod-builder with one of the more difficult aspects of producing tapered strips.

Objective
To make bamboo rod construction splines in a faster and easier method than by use of a standard planning form and hand plane.

Concept
The physical acts involved in planing a spline by hand to a desired taper are revised to adapt the dimensioning of the bamboo to machine planing as follows:

1. Instead of moving the hand plane along the strip held in the planing form, the planing form itself is moved past the cutting blade of the planing device—in this case a router bit.
2. Instead of working on one strip at a time and making multiple cuts with a hand plane to bring the spline to finished dimensions, the machine is used to make fewer cuts on all of the strips in a rod section in each operating cycle (setup).
3. Each strip, rather than being held in the planing form by hand pressure, is held in the form at the point of cutting by the spring-loaded pressure rollers located on each side of the router bit.
4. The depth of cutting with the standard form is regulated by the setting of the adjusting screws (either differential screws or push-pull type). Whereas with the machine planing device, the depth of each series of cuts is set and controlled by the positioning of the roller fence and measured accurately by the installed dial indicator gauge. Each set of cuts is made on all six (6) strips and then the fence is quickly and precisely set for the next set of cuts by use of the hand-screw knob which is then locked in position again.
5. The planing form used with this machine is of conventional style with two caveats:
    A: All adjusting screws (push-pull type) must be located on the top side of the form (see drawing and photo) to provide for a smooth bottom surface to rest upon and move along the machine's table.
    B. The form should be of relatively lightweight construction to facilitate its movement. Maple or aluminum may be used.

Design Philosophy
This machine has been designed with four goals in mind:
1. Flexibility: To allow for the fabrication of the component assemblies to be made in various ways using alternative materials.
2. Common materials: To permit construction from materials that are readily available from local suppliers.
3. Simple construction: To design the machine in such a way as to permit construction using simple tools.
4. Low cost: To provide for an inexpensive yet functional tool.

In regards to these goals it is believed that the device can be built for a little over $100.00 U.S., aside from the cost of the router, dial indicator, planing form and electrical items. The necessary shop tools needed include: drills, files, hack saw, taps, dyes, etc. Access to a good drill press and table saw is highly desirable, and use of a metal lathe would be a luxury. Jack has access to a "non-ferrous metal cutting blade" for his table saw which was of great help in cutting the aluminum used in the machine construction. The metal shapes, screws, nuts, bolts and washers are all standard sizes. The ball bearings used can be any size close to that listed here. A good source for these is rollerblade skate bearings. Sets of sixteen are inexpensive and the right size too.

In summary, note that of this type machine can be made from a number of different materials and sizes to as may be required to suit the availability in the builders locale. A competent machinist should be able to make one in just a few hours, whereas the home-shop builder may take a bit more time.

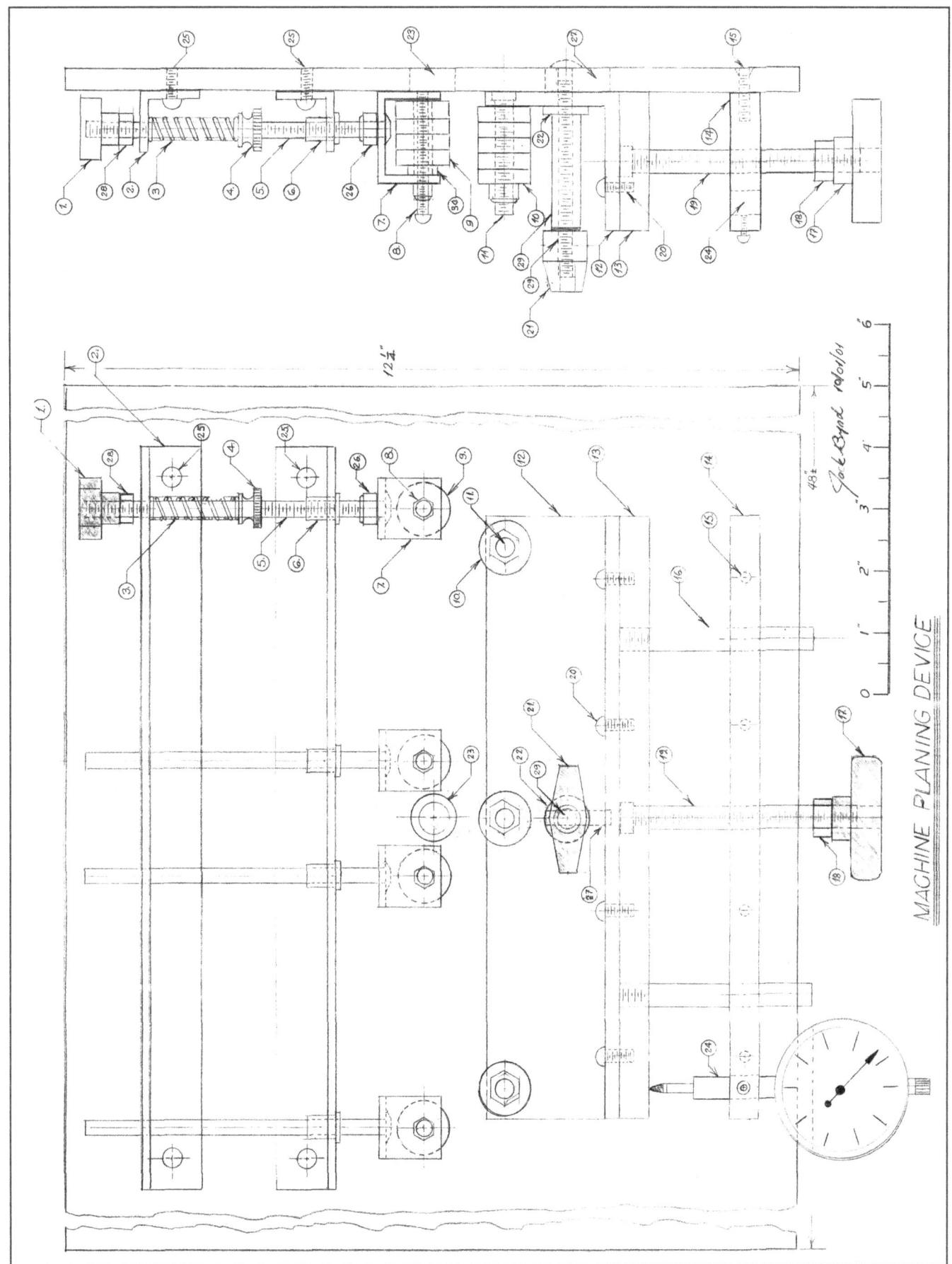

Fig. 7: Assembly drawing of Byrd's Machine Planing Device.

TIP NO. 4: BYRD'S MACHINE PLANING DEVICE

An assembly drawing of the machine planing device is shown in Fig. 7. Please note that this drawing does not show the planning form nor the router and router bit which are mounted from below.

Material list for the machine planing device by item number as shown on the assembly drawing

1. Plastic handles (4) with 1/4'-20NC inside threads.
2. Pressure roller bases (2) aluminum angle
   1/8" x 1" x 1" x 12" long.
3. Pressure roller springs (4) compression springs 5/16"i.d. x 3/8"o.d. x 1 1/2" long.
4. Spring-force adjusting knobs (4) knurled brass with 1/4"-20NC threaded bore.
5. Pressure roller shafts (4) steel carriage bolts 1/4"-20NC x 5" long.
6. Pressure roller-shaft bearings (4) flanged bronze bushings 1/4"i.d. x 3/8"o.d. x 1/2" long.
7. Pressure roller holders (4) aluminum channels 1/8" x 1 1/4" x 1" x 1" wide.
8. Bearing shafts (4) 5/16" x 1 1/2" roll pin.
9. Bearings (4 stacks of 4 ea.=16) skate ball bearings 22mm o.d. x 8mm bore x 7mm wide.
10. Rollers (3 stacks of 5 ea.=15) skate ball bearings 22mm o.d. x 8mm bore x 7mm wide.
11. Roller bolts (3) 5/16"-18NC x 1/2" long with lock nut.
12. Adjustable fence front plate and roller base (1) aluminum angle 1/4" x 2" x 2" x 8" long.
13. & 14. Fence back plates (2) aluminum bar 1/2" x 2" x 8" long.
15. Screws for securing fixed back plate to base (4) #10-32 x 1 3/4" long flat head machine screws.
16. Guide rods (2) brass rods 3/8" x 3" long threaded on end.
17. Knurled knob for adjusting bolt on fence with 3/8"— 24NF bore.
18. Lock nut 3/8"—24NF.
19. Fence adjusting bolt (1) 3/8"—24NF x 3" long (head turned circular).
20. Screws for floating back plate to angle (4) #10-32 x 3/4" long round head machine screws.
21. Lock handle with 1/4"—20NC female thread.
22. Washer.
23. Clearance hole for router bit.
24. Dial indicator with 0.001" graduations and 1" travel, lock in position with #6-32 x 1/2" long machine screw.
25. Screws for pressure roller bases (8) #10-32 x 3/4" long round head machine screws.
26. & 28. Lock nuts for pressure rollers shafts (8) 1/4"—20NC hex nuts
27. Slot 1/4"x 1 1/8" in base for locking bolt.
29. Adjustment lock shaft (1) carriage bolt 1/4"x 20NC x 3" long, with locking sleeve 1/4"id. x 1/2"od.x 2" long.

The following photographs Fig. 8 and Fig. 9 show the machine planing device in use.

Fig. 8: Byrd's Machine Planing Device without planing form in place.

Fig. 9: Byrd's Machine Planing Device with planing form and bamboo strip.

The Byrd Machine Planing Device may also be fitted with a special angle bracket accessory in order to cut a 60°-angle on the bamboo strip. The cane spline is held firmly in position by pressure rollers while the vertical router bit cuts one side. This is one of the key roughing steps in preparing the spline for tapering. See Fig. 10.

Climb Cut Versus Conventional Cut

At recent gatherings of bamboo fly-rod builders, when spline

Fig. 10: Byrd's machine planing device with accessory bracket for angle cutting.

milling or planing machines have been discussed, the term "climb cut" is often heard. Sometimes there seems to be confusion as to exactly what the term means.

Consider a router bit rotating in a counterclockwise direction: A climb cut exists when the material being cut moves in the same direction as the cutting edge of the router bit. See Fig. 11.

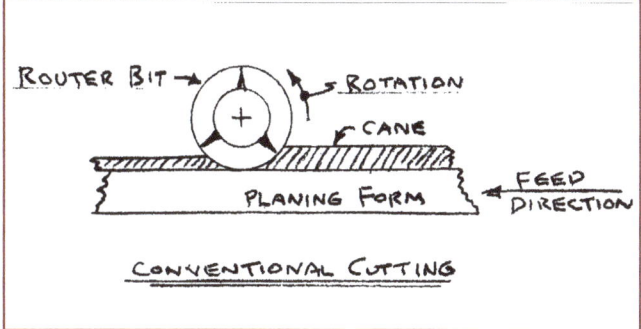

Fig. 11: Climb cutting setup.

A conventional cut exists when the material moves in the opposite direction to the cutting edge of the router bit. See Fig. 12.

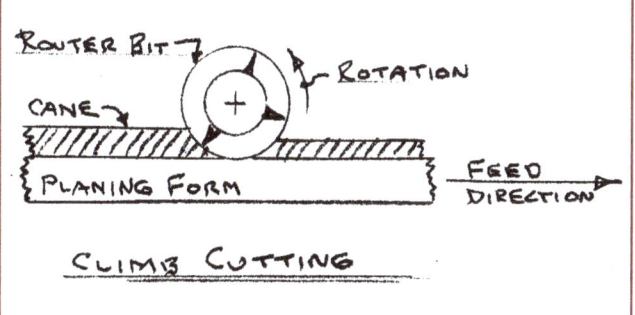

Fig. 12: Conventional cutting setup.

With the Byrd Machine Planing Device either the conventional or climb cut may be used. The advantage of a conventional cut is that you can attain very good control of the speed when hand-feeding the planing form past the cutter. However, at fast router RPM's there is a tendency for friction burns to be made on the surface of the cane strips being cut. This can be overcome by reducing the speed of rotation of the router bit through the use of a rheostat with the router. Also, there is a tendency to produce chips and splinters on the spline surfaces, particularly when heavy cuts (0.030-0.050) are attempted. This in turn can be overcome by using a sanding drum instead of the carbide router bit, but there is some sacrifice in accuracy when this is done.

On the other hand, when climb cutting is used there is a strong tendency for the spline to be pulled in the direction of feeding. This reduces the ability to smoothly move the spline past the router bit and, in the extreme case, can shoot the spline out the end of the planing form in a dangerous manner. When the spline moves past the cutter in a jerky manner as occurs in this operation, grooves may be cut into the spline surface. The powerful pull by the router bit can be reduced, but not eliminated, by reducing the router RPM and by keeping the depth of cut small. The advantage of the climb cut is that it seems to eliminate the tendency to chip and splinter the spline during the milling operation. If climb cutting is used there are some special safety procedures that need to be followed:

1. Wear heavy gloves or other finger protection. The cane is very sharp and can severely cut one's hands.

2. Use a planing form that is long enough to be held in place by all the pressure rollers of the machine-planing device before cutting is started. Both hands will need to be fully employed in controlling the smooth travel of the planing form past the router bit.

3. Use a foot switch for router power. There are times when the router must be stopped or started without losing hold of the planing form with both hands.

Tip No. 5
Chamberlain Spline Milling Mechanism

This unique machine was designed and built by Theron Chamberlain, an excellent fly-fisherman, long-time friend and former member of the Northwest Fly Anglers Club of Seattle. He used his vast experience as a tool-design engineer for the Bendix Corp. in developing this equipment.

The basic system incorporated here is to use a horizontally mounted router to cut the cane strips as they are fed through the unit while being held in a planing form. A small, clear plastic cage (not shown) with a vacuum hose attached, is installed over the router cutter bit area to remove the dust and cuttings during operation. See Fig. 14.

The cane strip is held down in the planing form by two spring-loaded, ball-bearing pressure rollers. The router cutter is seen between the two pressure rollers and is driven by a speed-controlled router motor. The router cutter is a 3/4" diameter x 3 1/2" long with a 1/2"-diameter shank and rotates at about 15,000 RPM. The length of the cutter provides for some adjustment in and out to allow additional sharp cutting surfaces of the bit to be utilized. Note too that the vertical adjustment of the cutter is measured and set by using a dial indicator. See Fig. 15.

This machine has a powered two-direction feed mechanism actuated through a gear train. The v-grooved planing form has attached to it on the underside, a toothed gear rack. The power for traversing the planing form in the horizontal direction is provided by a 1/2 amp. barbeque motor. The speed of traverse is purposely slow at about 12"/minute. The photograph in Fig. 16 shows the gear train and the reversing lever as viewed from below.

The mounting of the router is accomplished using a metal face plate, a plastic plate spacer and a plywood angle bracket. The motor is spring-loaded from below by four (4) compression springs and is adjusted from above by way of a threaded

Fig. 15: Spline hold-down system.

Fig. 14: Chamberlain's Spline Milling Mechanism with the planing form and cane strip in position.

16 ❖ CANE RODS: TIPS & TAPERS

Fig. 17: Router motor mounting with Theron Chamberlain at the controls.

screw. Fig. 17 shows the router mounting with Theron Chamberlain at the controls.

Detailed drawings and the attendant bill of material are shown in the three drawings on pages 18-20:

Fig. 16: Chamberlain's Spline Milling Mechanism gear train and reversing gear.

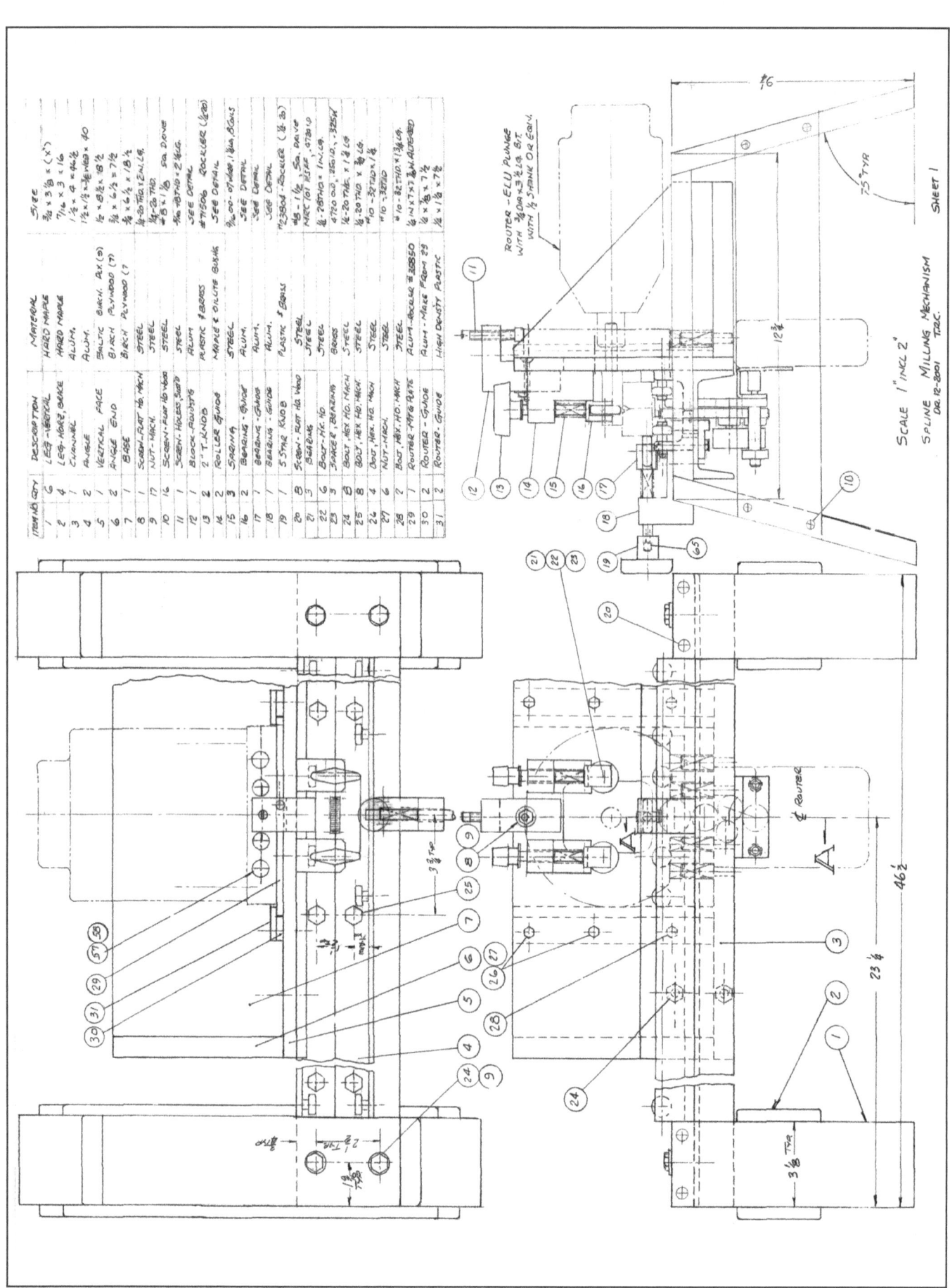

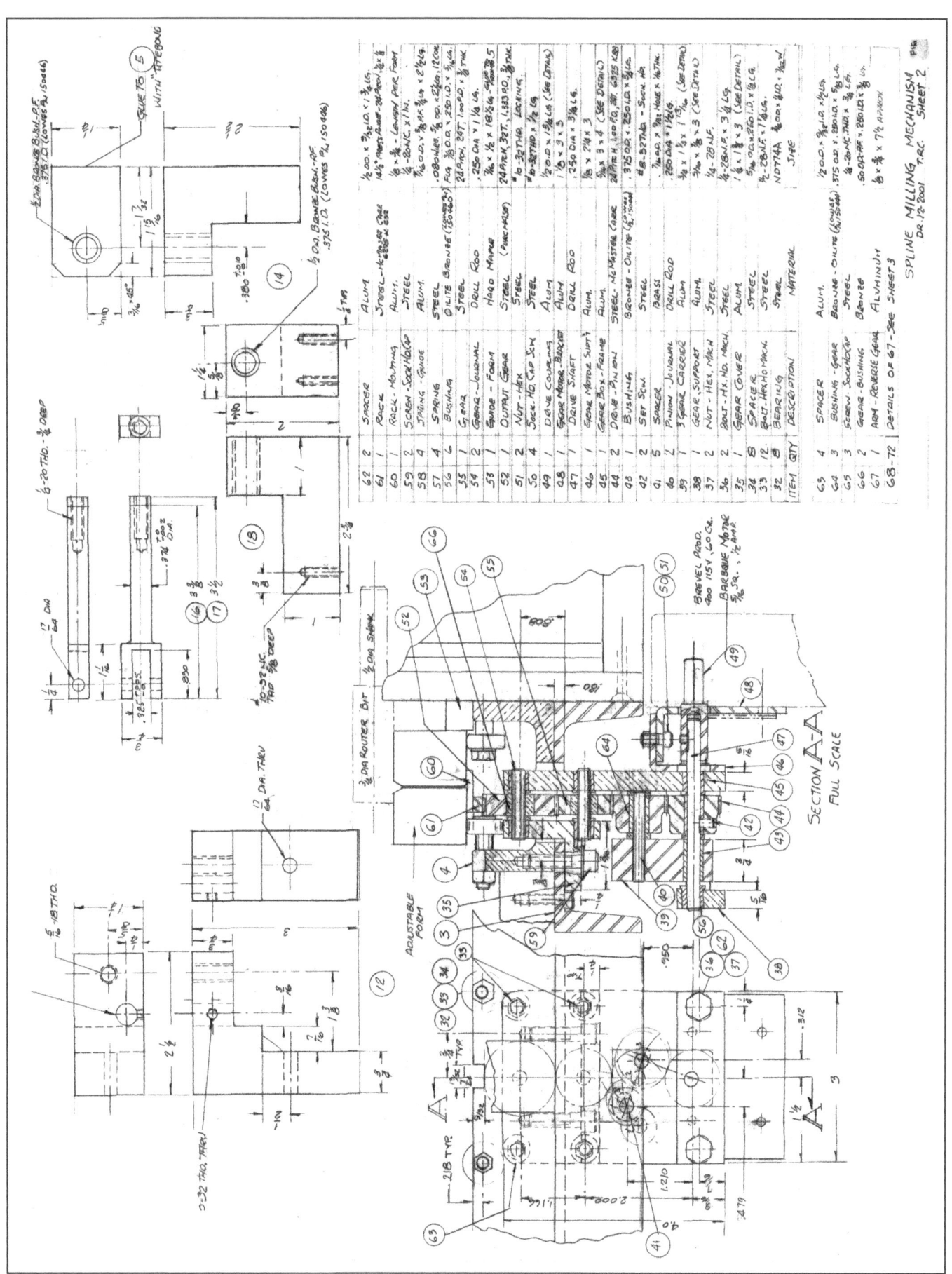

Tip No. 5: Chamberlain Spline Milling Mechanism

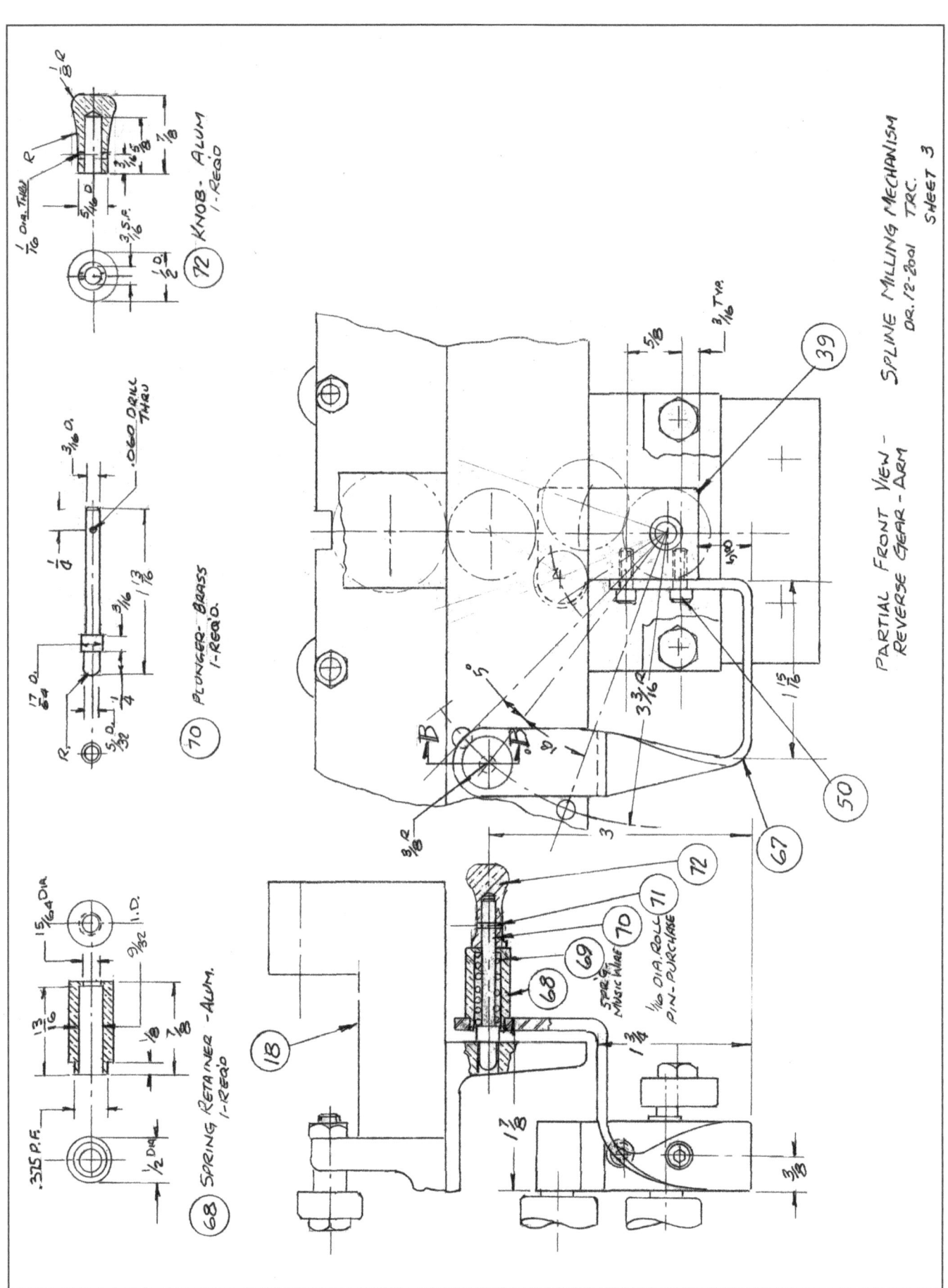

Tip No. 6
The Tensioner

The purpose of this simple but extremely effective device is to straighten and untwist a freshly glued-up rod section and to hold it straight while the glue dries. See Figs. 21 & 22.

Simplicity in design is a major feature of this unit. All of the parts can readily be attained from local hardware stores and tool suppliers.

Bill of Materials:
1. Steel channel = one (1) pc. 1 1/2" x 3/4" x 72" long "Kindorf Channel" found in the electrical section of a hardware store
2. Drill chucks = two (2) Jacobs 2B threaded in the bore with 5/16"-24 threads per inch (national fine), and one (1) Jacob 33B threaded 5/16"–24 NF
3. Threaded rods = two (2) steel threaded rods 5/16"x 24 NF threads/inch x 10" long
4. Hex nuts = four (4) 5/16"-24NF steel hex nuts
5. Washers = four (4) 5/16" flat steel washers
6. Lag screws = two steel lag screws with washers (not shown in photo) used to fasten the wood blocks to the steel channel from underneath

Only basic shop tools are necessary for its assembly.

Instructions for Use:
1. Position the two drill chucks on the steel channel to match the length of the rod section. Note: the Jacobs 33B chuck has a larger bore in the chuck jaws than the 2B and can be used to handle butt sections of larger thickness.
2. Glue up a rod section and bind with string in a binding machine.
3. Place the newly glued-up rod section in the tensioner and tighten the drill chucks.
4. Place a little tension on the rod section by tightening the 5/16" hex nuts on the outer ends of the wood blocks.
5. Sight down one flat of the rod to determine if it has any twists in it. If so, remove the twist by rotating one chuck while the other chuck is locked in position so that it will not rotate.
6. Sight down the rod section again to see if there are any bends in the rod section. Deflect the section carefully in a direction opposite to the bend. Take great care in this step so as not to put a kink in the rod section.
7. Once the rod section is straight, place more tension on the rod and lock all four (4) hex nuts.
8. Sight down the rod section one final time to be certain it is still straight.
9. Let the rod section dry overnight (12 hours preferred) at room temperature.
10. Then carefully remove the rod section from the tensioner without bending or twisting it.
11. Hang the rod section (still in the string binding) in a rod-drying cabinet for an additional 12 hours at 110-120°F.

Fig. 21: Tensioner assembly.

Fig. 22: Tensioner double-chuck detail.

Tip No. 7
Ferrules

Preparing ferrules for mounting on a rod is one of the most important steps in rod building or repairing. A properly-prepared ferrule will prevent the age-old problem of developing "thread cracking" in the wrapping at the end of the ferrule. The following is a step-by-step procedure detailing how to v-notch a ferrule and install it on a six-sided rod:

Thin down the end of the ferrule from the outboard edge for the depth of the serration so that the metal comes to a paper-thin end. This can be accomplished by hand grinding or by filing it while mounted in a lathe as shown in Fig. 23.

Fig. 23: Thinned-down ferrule.

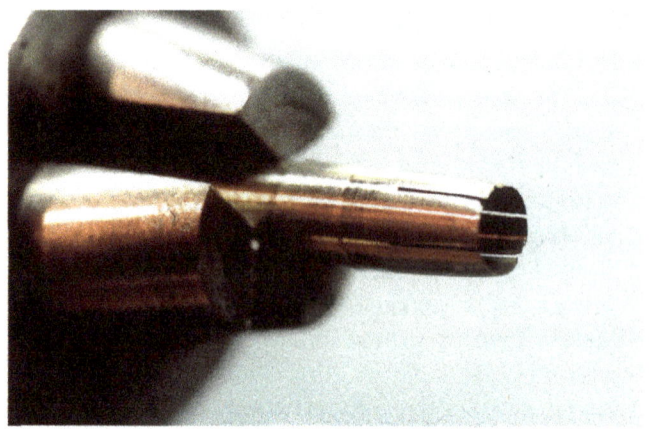

The next operation is to V-notch the ferrule. An excellent way to do this is to use a Dremel grinder equipped with a Dremel 7120 diamond disc point bit. This cutter is 17/64" in diameter with a 3/32"-diameter arbor, and is made of steel tipped with diamond particles. See Fig. 24.

Fig. 24: Dremel #7120 diamond disc point bit.

Next mount the Dremel grinder to the work bench in such a way as to free up both of your hands for cutting the v-notches in the ferrule. A simple C-clamp arrangement will do nicely. Hold the ferrule under the diamond disc so that the disc's cutting edge lines up with a serration as shown in Fig. 25.

Fig. 25: Cutting the V-notches.

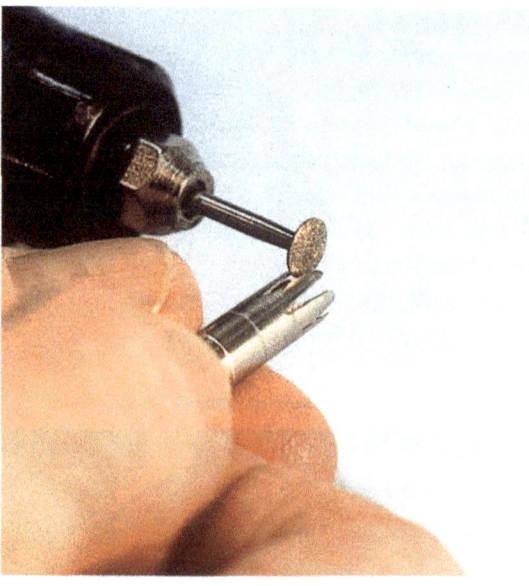

Cut the V-notches so that the each V-groove is about as deep as the serration is cut in the ferrule. Great care must be taken not to deform the end of the ferrule during this operation since the metal is paper-thin at the end of the ferrule and will bend easily. The final result will be a V-notched ferrule ready to install on the cane rod.

To install the ferrule on the rod, clean the bore of the ferrule and mount it on the rod using urethane bond adhesive (U-Bond). Position the ferrule so that the serrations line up with the corners of the hexagonal bamboo rod and so that the points of the V-notches are in the center of the each of the flats. See Fig. 26. Then bind the ferrule tightly with string until the glue dries. Once the glue is dry, carefully remove the binding string being certain not to pull the ferrule tabs loose from the bamboo. Then remove any excess glue using 0000 steel wool, polishing in one direction off the end of the ferrule and towards the cane. Polishing in this way will also help to prevent lifting the ferrule tabs loose.

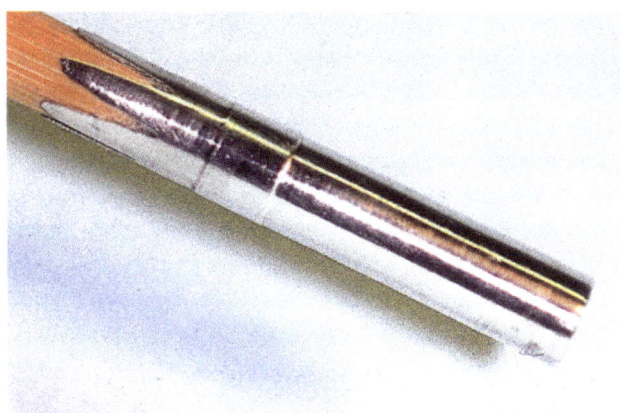

Fig. 26: Notched ferrule positioned on rod.

Ferrule Types

Ferrules of several different styles and materials are available and many, which are no longer mass produced today, are still seen on older rods. For low-cost, inexpensive rods that are being repaired, chrome or nickel-plated brass ferrules are often used. One supplier of this type of ferrule is E.J. Hille, The Angler's Supply House. But note that this type of ferrule is not serrated. It is important to recognize that some of the better-quality mass-produced rods of the past (such as Wright & McGill and Heddon) were indeed furnished with better-quality ferrules and those can usually be reused.

Nickel silver type ferrules have been made by a number of companies including: Orvis, Super Z, Uslan, Leonard, Joe's Tackle, Classic Sporting Enterprises, Rodon, Cortland, and Rod & Gun (stainless steel), and R.E.C, and Bellinger.

Orvis ferrules, although well made, were not serrated and were "stepped down" in the bore of the male half. This design did, however, allow the ferrule to be used equally well on quadrate rods. The later models had clear plastic moisture dams inside the female half requiring great care especially when using heat when installing or removing them. Orvis ferrules, and a number of others, are no longer made today, however independent craftsmen can reproduce a suitable copy.

One of the best and most famous ferrules was the Super Z produced by Louis Feierabend in the 1940s. These nickel silver ferrules were serrated and designed with a high section modulus (an abbreviation for this term in engineering parlance is "Z," hence its name) to provide strength where it was needed the most and eliminated the "step down" bore problem. It is easy to identify one of these ferrules since they are stamped with a logo consisting of the word "Super" with an oversized "Z" through the center of it. Super Zs were used by Garrison, Gillum, Young, Uslan and even Orvis (on some models). The patent rights to the Super Z were eventually sold to Conolon, a fiberglass-rod producer who in turn sold out to the Garcia Corp., who then sold the patent rights to Rodon. After that, the Cortland Line Co. acquired Rodon so that to this day descendants of the Super Z are still being produced.

Most rod-builders today use the Super Swiss ferrule made by Classic Sporting Enterprises, the nickel silver ferrule sold by the Research Engineering Co. (REC) or they make their own. My preference is to be sure that the ferrule is made with soldered joints and not assembled with "Loctite" cement.

Ferrule Size Selection

Picking the right-size ferrule is an important step in building or repairing a bamboo rod. If the ferrule chosen is too small in diameter too much of the outer power fibers of the cane must be removed, resulting in a weak spot doomed to failure. On the other hand, if the ferrule selected is too large then it is necessary to build up the cane where the ferrule will be placed resulting in unnecessary work and additional rod weight and stiffness. The following chart (Fig. 27) is designed to give the optimum-size ferrule for a six (6)-sided hexagonal bamboo rod. Note that in other chapters of this book, charts will be found for quadrate (4-sided) and pentagonal (5-sided) rods.

Fig. 27: Optimum ferrule size for hexagonal bamboo rod.

Minimum "d" dimension thickness across the flats in inches	Maximum "d" dimension thickness across the flats in inches	Ferrule size (bore of the male slide)
0.125	0.141	9/64"
0.142	0.156	10/64"
0.157	0.172	11/64"
0.173	0.187	12/64"
0.188	0.203	13/64"
0.204	0.219	14/64"
0.220	0.234	15/64"
0.235	0.250	16/64"
0.251	0.265	17/64"
0.266	0.281	18/64"
0.282	0.297	19/64"
0.298	0.313	209/64"

Bluing Ferrules

Bluing or blackening ferrules has been done for many years. Some say the purpose was to prevent the ferrule from flashing or glinting in the sunlight thus scaring away wary trout at the trout stream. For bluing ferrules made of nickel silver, several liquids are available. Included are Birchwood Casey Perma Blue and one made by Metal Bluing products. These work fairly well but tend to leave flakey and uneven coatings which do not adhere well.

The best oxidizer I have found is called Payne's Original Formula Nickel Silver Oxidizer sold by The Fly Rod and Room (see Fig. 28). The instructions for its use are simple and easy to follow. Polish the surface to be blued with 0000 steel wool and then clean it with thinner or denatured alcohol to remove any oils or grease. Dip the ferrule for 30 seconds or so, rinse with water and dry. If one dipping does not darken the surface quite enough, a second exposure to the liquid will do the trick.

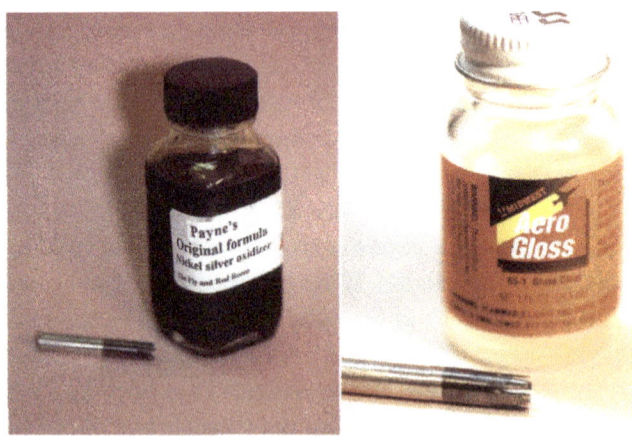

Fig. 28, 29: Bluing liquid & bluing protective coating.

To protect the blued surface from future damage it is best to coat it with lacquer or, even better, is the model airplane hot fuel dope Aero Gloss (see Fig. 29). This material is available at most local hobby shops.

For brass ferrules a liquid called Brass Black by Birchwood Casey does a suitable job. Note that it contains selenium dioxide, which is poisonous if swallowed. To use this material, clean the surface to be blackened with denatured alcohol or a cleaner-degreaser, then rinse with water and dry. Brighten the area to be blackened with 0000 steel wool to remove any surface oxides, then rinse and dry again. Apply the material with a swab, let it sit for one minute, then rinse with cold water and dry. Polish with a clean dry cloth. Repeat the treatment if a darker color is desired. Coat the surface with gun wax to protect it.

Ferrule Plugs

An extra refinement sometimes offered with cane rods is ferrule plugs. These devices are meant to keep dust and dirt out from the female ferrule bore so that the close tolerances of the fit are not compromised when the rod is assembled. The plugs can be made from plastic, aluminum or wood with a cork sleeve. Fig. 30 shows a sketch of the ferrule plug and Fig. 31 shows the dimensions of cork-lined wood plugs for a range of ferrule sizes.

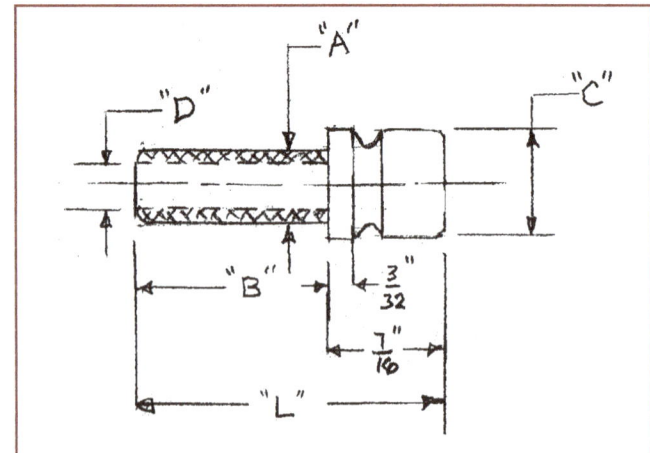

Fig. 30: Rosewood ferrule plug with cork sleeve.

Fig. 31: Ferrule plug dimension for super Swiss ferrules.

Ferrule Size	O.D. male slide in inches	O.D. of cork plug dimension "A" inches	Length of cork plug dimension "B" inches	Plug Range O.D. dimension "C" inches	Plug wood core O.D. dimension "D" inches	Overall length inches
10	0.188	0.190/0.192	0.5	2.555	0.100	15/16
11			0.5	0.275	0.100	15/16
12	0.218	0.220/0.222	0.625	0.300	0.125	1 1/16
13	0.233	0.235/0.237	0.625	0.300	0.150	1 1/16
14	0.246	0.248/0.250	0.750	0.335	0.150	1 3/16
15	0.265	0.267/0.269	0.750	0.335	0.150	1 3/16
16	0.281	0.283/0.285	0.750	0.350	0.150	1 3/16
17	0.298	0.300/0.302	0.750	0.375	0.150	1 3/16
18	0.312	0.314/0.316	0.750	0.390	0.150	1 3/16
19	0.327	0.329/0.331	0.750	0.400	0.150	1 3/16

Tip No. 8
Guide Spacing

Fig. 32: Guide spacing for 2-piece rods.

Sta	Distance from small end of section	Guide size
	5 ft. x 2 pc.	
1	3.5	2/0
2	8.5	1/0
3	13.6875	1/0
4	19.75	1/0
5	26.875	1
6	3.4375	8mm
Sta	**6 ft. x 2 pc.**	
1	4.0	2/0
2	10.0	1/0
3	17.0	1/0
4	25.0	1
5	33.25	2
6	5.9375	8mm
Sta	**6 1/ ft. x 2 pc.**	
1	4.5	2/0
2	11	1/0
3	18.25	1/0
4	26	1/0
5	34.625	1
6	2.375	2
7	12.75	8mm
Sta	**7 ft. x 2 pc.**	
1	4.5	2/0
2	10.25	1/0
3	16.5	1/0
4	23.25	1/0
5	30.5	1
6	38.25	1
7	5	2
8	14.25	8mm
Sta	**7 1/2 ft. x 2 pc.**	
1	4.375	2/0
2	9.75	1/0
3	15.5	1/0
4	21.626	1/0
5	28.125	1
6	35	1
7	42.25	2
8	5.375	3
9	16.5	8mm
Sta	**7 3/4 ft. x 2 pc.**	
1	4.375	2/0
2	9.75	1/0
3	15.5	1/0
4	21.625	1/0
5	28.125	1
6	35	1
7	442.1875	2
8	4.125	3
9	14.5	8mm
Sta	**8 ft. x 2 pc.**	
1	4.875	2/0
2	10.5	1/0
3	16	1/0
4	21.75	1/0
5	27.75	1
6	34.25	1
7	41.5	2
8	4.5	3
9	19.375	10mm
Sta	**8 1/4 ft. x 2 pc.**	
1	4.875	2/0
2	10.875	1/0
3	17.375	1/0
4	24.25	1/0
5	31.25	1
6	38.5	1
7	46.625	2
8	6.75	3
9	19	10mm
Sta	**8 1/2 ft. x 2 pc.**	
1	4.875	2/0
2	10.875	1/0
3	17.375	1/0
4	24.125	1/0
5	31.125	1
6	38.375	1
7	45.875	2
8	4	2
9	12.5	3
10	21.875	10mm
Sta	**9 ft. x 2 pc.**	
1	5.5	2/0
2	11.75	1/0
3	18.25	1/0
4	25	1
5	32	1
6	39.5	2
7	47.125	2
8	2.5	3
9	11.75	8mm
10	22.75	10mm
Sta	**7 1/2 ft. x 3 pc.**	
1	4.5	2/0
2	9.875	1/0
3	15.75	1/0
4	21.75	1/0
5	28	1
6	5.5	1
7	12.5	2
8	20.375	3
9	3	8mm
Sta	**8 ft. x 3 pc.**	
1	4.375	2/0
2	9.75	1/0
3	15.5	1/0
4	21.625	1/0
5	28.125	1/0
6	4.5	1
7	10.625	1
8	18.25	1
9	26.5	2
10	5.375	10mm
Sta	**8 1/2 ft. x 3 pc.**	
1	5.125	2/0
2	10.5	1/0
3	16.25	1/0
4	22.75	1
5	30	1
6	2.75	1
7	11.125	2
8	19.625	2
9	29	3
10	6.375	10mm
Sta	**9 ft. x 3 pc.**	
1	5.5	2/0
2	11.75	1/0
3	18.25	1/0
4	25	1/0
5	32	1
6	3.5	1
7	11.25	1
8	19.25	2
9	28.5	3
10	5.5625	10mm

Tip No. 9
Grips

here doesn't seem to be any standard for grip names, dimensions or sizes. Some of the more common names for grips include:

- Cigar
- Thompson (similar to Half Wells)
- Standard (similar to Half Wells)
- Ritz
- Fishtail (similar to Full Wells)
- Philippe Cigar
- Full Wells
- Gordon (a straight taper front to rear)
- Half Wells
- Perfectionist (similar to Half Wells)
- Tear Drop
- Reversed Half Wells
- Comficient (a grooved grip)
- Garrison (slightly tapered front to rear)
- Torpedo
- Coke Bottle
- Western (similar to Reversed half Wells)
- Mild Reversed Half Wells
- Thumb Cutout (seen on South bend rods with Comficient Grip)

Some of the most commonly used grips are variations of the Cigar, Wells or the Garrison. Approximate dimensions for four of these are:

Fig. 35: Cigar grip.

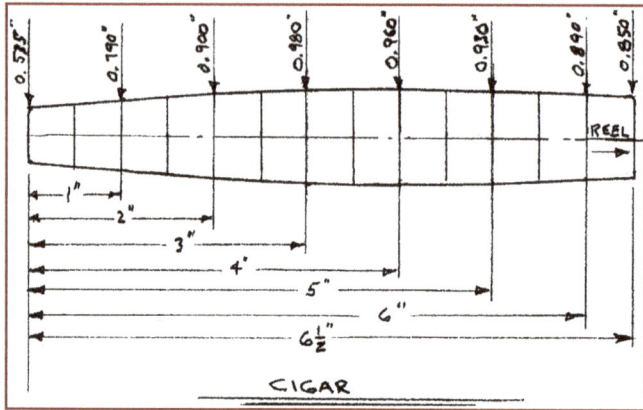

Fig. 36 Full Wells grip.

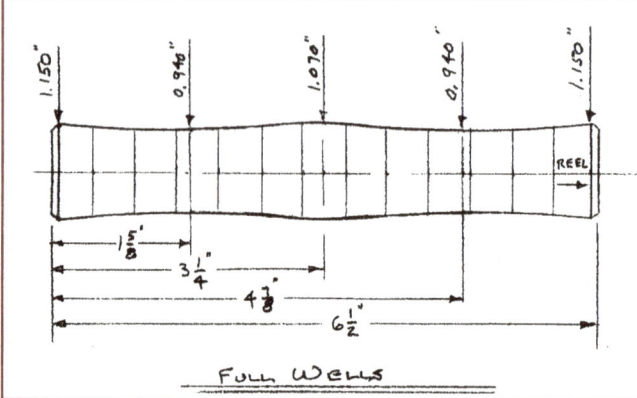

Fig. 37: Reversed half Wells.

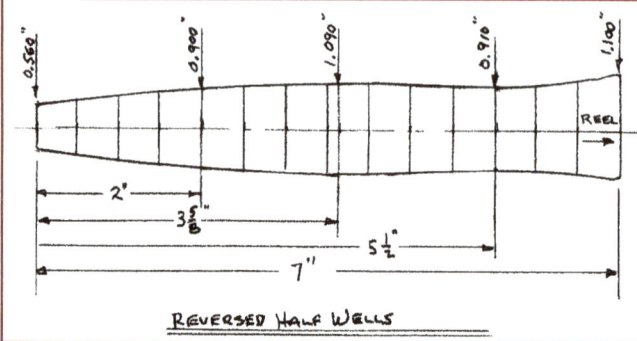

Fig. 34: Sample of some grip shapes.

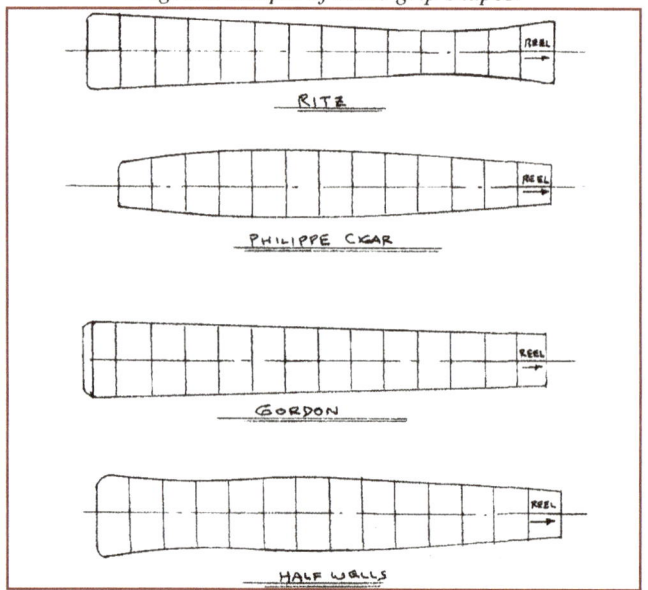

26 ● Cane Rods: Tips & Tapers

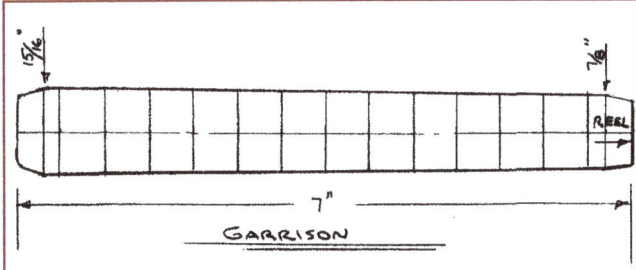

Fig. 38: Garrison grip.

The factors to consider in selecting which grip design and dimensions to use on a particular rod should include:

- The size of the hand using the rod.
- The purchaser's desire (if known).
- Comfort.
- Grip length.
- Balance.
- The size of the fly rod: short rods generally have shorter grip length while Spey rods have longer grips.
- Whether or not there should be room to slide the hand along the grip for individual adjustment.
- Two-handed or single-handed rod.

- Fighting butt extension option.
- Foregrip option.
- Maker's preference.

RECOMMENDATIONS FOR GRIP CONSTRUCTION:
First and foremost, use the very best grade cork. Its appearance alone provides a quality upgrade to the rod. Then with the grip use an attractive winding check and reel seat. Nickel silver trim adds substantially to the elegance of the finished product. Glue the corks together using Elmer's Carpenters glue. This can be done either on the rod blank or (as is my preference) on a 1/4"-diameter steel rod mandrel. Glue the cork to the rod using U-Bond urethane adhesive as this will expand to fill any voids. Rough the cork grip to shape using 100-grit sandpaper, saving the cork dust created. Fill any holes in the cork surface with a mixture of cork dust, Duco Household cement and a little titanium dioxide (to whiten it). Then finish sanding the grip using 220-grit sandpaper. The finish must be uniform in color and silky smooth to the touch. If a Garrison or Cigar style of grip is used, make the grip 7 inches long so as to provide the caster with room to move the casting hand along the grip to find the place that provides the best comfort, power and balance.

Fig. 39: Example of a Comficient Grip with thumb cutout.

TIP NO. 9: GRIPS ● 27

Tip No. 10
Rod Wrapping

Simplicity is the key to having a good rod wrapper. The unit shown in Fig. 40 and Fig. 41 is one that is easy to build in the home workshop. Notice that the rod is held down in the v-grooves by the 16-ounce lead weight leaving both hands free to rotate the rod and handle the thread. It also demonstrates the advantage of being able to wrap with the thread between the two stands, or to cantilever the rod out over the end by moving the sliding thread stand outside the sliding v-grooved stand. This arrangement allows wrapping closer to the end of a rod section, such as when doing ferrule wraps.

Fig. 40: Wrapping between the stands.

Fig. 41: Wrapping with the rod cantilevered.

A sketch showing the main dimensions for this rod wrapper and its bill of materials is provided in Fig. 42.

- 6 ft of 1x4 (3/4 x 3 1/2 actual size) fir, spruce, hemlock or maple.
- One (1) 1/4"-20NC x 6" long steel-threaded rod.

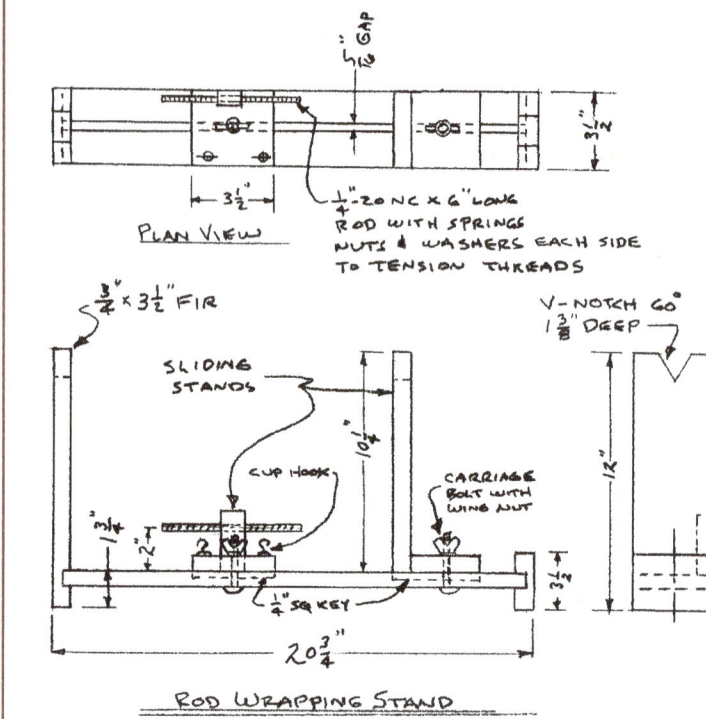

Fig. 42: Sketch of rod wrapper and its bill of materials.

- Six (6) 1/4" washers.
- Two (2) 1/4" 20NC hex nuts.
- Two (2) 1/4" 20 NC hex lock nuts.
- Two (2) 1/4" i.d. x 3/4" long compression springs.
- Two (2) 5/16" 18NC x 2" long carriage bolts with nuts and washers.
- Two (2) cup hooks.
- One (1) 16 oz. lead weight with string to hang it.

Color Sticks

Here's a unique idea to assure getting the correct and desired wrap color. Take a section of rod blank and wrap a guide on it with each available color of thread. Then mark the thread identification next to the wrap and varnish the wrap. In some cases it may be appropriate to apply color preserver to the thread prior to varnishing and if that is done, mark it as such. Use both silk and nylon threads. Now when making a custom rod the purchaser can select exactly which wrap he or she desires and will see the color after it is varnished while making their decision. See Fig. 43.

Fig. 43: Color stick.

Tipping

An easy way to make narrow tipping wraps is to use a fine thread. Eight ought (8/0) or six ought (6/0) both work quite nicely. Six turns of thread for the tipping will still produce a narrow band but still allow the ends to be pulled under and cut off without difficulty. Many fly-tying threads will suit this purpose.

Invisible Wraps

Making truly invisible wraps is a bit of a chore but here are some ways to do it:

Dwight Lyons, whose work with invisible wraps I admire, uses Pearsall's straw size 6/0. He applies Flexcoat for the beginning application working it in with his fingers and then uses polyurethane for the final coats. The wraps are then rubbed down with rottenstone as needed to smooth them out, and colored with an artist's marking pen or permanent shoe polish if needed to match a tan or brown shade of cane.

Another trick is to use a fine artist liner brush and put a drop of thinned finish down the "tunnel" next to the guide foot after the guide is wrapped, but before the thread finish is applied. Several applications may be required to fill the air pocket and wick some finish along the guide finish. Slightly thinning and heating the finish is recommended by Pearsall's and does seem to help.

Using tan nylon thread #290 on cane that is on the brownish side produces a transparent wrap when varnished matching the color of the bamboo.

Tip No. 11
Maker's Label

There are several nice ways for rod-builders to use in marking their rods for identification. Just as important as the maker's name is the model name and line size. Here are some examples as to how rod-maker's have labeled their rods.

Seat Stamping
Hardy's in England marks the companies name and the serial number by stamping the metal reel seat. See Fig. 44. They also marked the rod model using black ink on the butt section. Some of their rods were marked with the ink-work arranged in a spiral pattern.

Fig. 44: Hardy reel seat stamping.

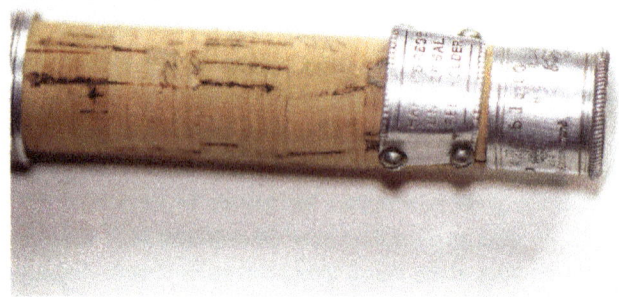

The Orvis Company did things a little differently by marking the butt section with the model and serial number, and also marked the other sections of the rod with the serial number. In addition, for some models, Orvis stamped the model, length, line size and serial number on a distinctive green and silver foil decal affixed to the aluminum rod case.

Leonard rods can be initially identified by their special aluminum tube fitted with brass caps, as well as by their green cloth rod bag. Leonard metal-stamped the reel seat and pocket cap on many of their models with the company name and tournament model. Then too, Leonard rods had a tag attached to the rod bag indicating the model and rod length.

South Bend was one of several rod companies that used decals and black ink-work on the butt section to label their rods. On the models equipped with a special ventilated grip and thumb cutout, a special silver-colored decal was positioned right in the thumb cutout. See Fig. 39 shown in Tip No. 9: Grips.

Ink-work
Heddon used extensive black ink-work on the butt section, including the company name written in a spiral fashion and on a separate flat showed the model, length, ferrule size and line size. On this particular rod's ink-work, the "#10" is the model number, the number "2 1/2" is the ferrule size, and the "HCH or D" is the line size (old designation). See Fig. 45.

Fig. 45: Heddon ink-work.

Rod-Case Marking
Heddon also used a distinctive aluminum rod case for some of its models, exhibiting a notched case cap that was stamped bearing the company name and location. See Fig. 46.

Fig. 46: Heddon rod case cap.

Signature Wraps
Many rod-makers used signature wraps as an identification system. These are a series of narrow wraps near the cork grip

arranged in a pattern specific to that maker. Oftentimes these were used in conjunction with a decal identifying the rod model. An example of this technique is shown for a Montague Splitswitch in Fig. 47.

Fig. 47: Montague splitswitch.

Two companies come to mind who used white ink rather than black. They are Horrocks Ibbotson and Edwards.

Tips for Doing Ink-Work

There are some tricks to bear in mind when doing ink-work on a cane rod:
• Practice on a scrap rod section.
• Polish the flat where the ink-work will be placed.
• Coat that area with a single coat of varnish and dry it thoroughly.
• Use India ink and a very finely-pointed nib. Use an old-fashioned pen holder with a removable point such as a #102 or #107 Speedball Artists' Pen with a super-fine point. See Fig. 48.
• Strive to attain a fine line with the ink. It looks better.
• Dry the ink thoroughly.
• Paint over the ink with a coat of varnish.
• If the ink-work is not satisfactory, remove it using 0000 steel wool and do it over again.

Fig. 48: Pen and ink.

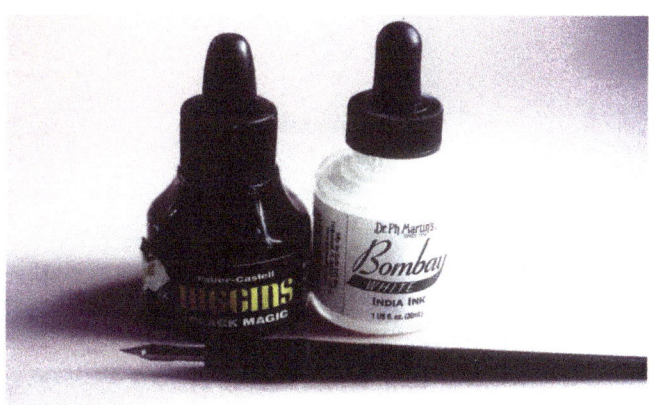

Pocket-Cap Stamping

Permanently marking the pocket cap or end plate with metal stamping is a lasting method of providing identification as to the maker. This service can be professionally provided by a local trophy or engraving shop. See Fig. 49.

Fig. 49: The author's butt-cap engraving.

Tip No. 11: Maker's Label ❋ 31

Finishing and Gluing

There seems to be little doubt that the most common finish for cane rods is varnish. But there's varnish, and then there's varnish. Over the years, three general camps have developed. One group prefers a tung oil varnish, one a spar varnish and yet another a polyurethane varnish. Each group has its reasons for selecting their favorite. At a Corbett Lake bamboo-rod-builders workshop, the attendees ranked the factors in order of importance as follows:

1. Water resistance
2. Adhesion
3. Durability
4. Effect on action
5. Appearance
6. Toxicity
7. Ease of application
8. Flexibility
9. Repairability

Another factor not taken into account is simply the availability of the product locally. All of the varnishes do seem to offer a degree of protection, especially if a coat or two of paraffin wax is applied afterwards. After twenty-four years of experience the author agrees with Everett Garrison that the best varnish is a polyurethane, preferably Pratt and Lambert R-10 gloss.

Other finishes are available however and, while not traditional, will produce a satisfactory coating. Consider for example epoxy, Clearthane (by Jessops), Pro-Fin, 100% Tung Oil, Sea-Fin teak oil or impregnation with a bakelite resin.

Impregnating

Two well-known rod-making companies that impregnated some of their rods are Orvis and Leonard. The Orvis Company obtained a patent by Wes Jordan, a famous rod-maker in the mid 1940s, for the process. A heat-hardening liquid phenol formaldehde resin produced by Union Carbide under the designation of Bakelite XC-16562 was used to cement their rod sections together, and a similar resin Bakelite BR-9651 was used for impregnating. The process is rather daunting, including equipment to soak the strips and temperature-controlled ovens for curing them.

The advantage of this coating system is that it provided a permanent finish requiring only cleaning and rubbing down. The disadvantage is that the impregnation increased the weight of the cane rod by about ten percent (10%). Another factor that might be called both an advantage and a disadvantage is that the impregnating process turned the cane dark. Some people like this color, others do not.

The Leonard Rod Company also produced a line of impregnated rods known as Duracane. This occurred during the mid-1960s and was marketed as a lower-priced line. While their system was similar to Orvis's, the color of the cane was lighter.

Varnish Thickness

An often-discussed topic with cane rods is the thickness of the varnish. This arises because rod-builders measure up rods they admire by other builders and need to deduct the varnish thickness to determine the actual taper. To produce an accurate answer, the author executed the following test: A sixteen-inch (10") long cane rod uncoated butt section was marked off by flat number in each of nine (9) stations along its length at one-inch (1") intervals. Each flat was numbered 1, 2, 3 and each station marked A, B, C, D, E, F, G, H, I. See Fig. 50.

Fig. 50: Varnish thickness test piece.

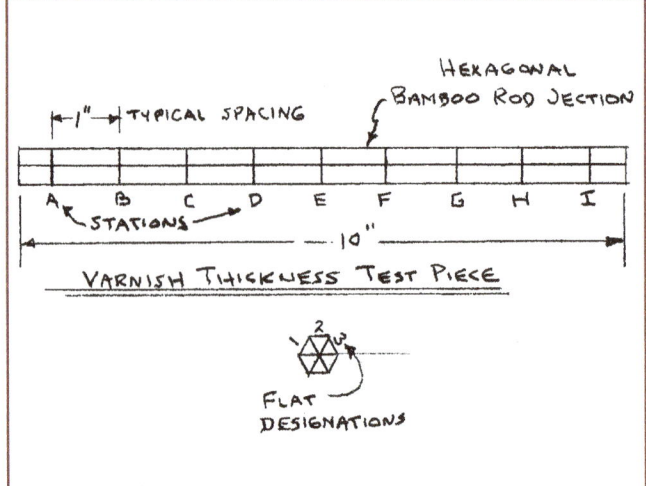

The test section (not one of mine) was then measured with a micrometer before varnishing, again after one coat of varnish and finally after two coats of varnish. The varnish used was Pratt and Lamberts R-10 Polyurethane applied at room temperature by dipping and dried eight (8) hours between coats at 110°F. See Fig. 51.

32 ❖ Cane Rods: Tips & Tapers

Before Varnish	Station A	Station B	Station C	Station D	Station E	Station F	Station G	Station H	Station I
Flat 1	0.364	0.365	0.366	0.363	0.369	0.369	0.370	0.372	0.373
Flat 2	0.354	0.355	0.363	0.364	0.363	0.364	0.367	0.365	0.360
Flat 3	0.359	0.364	0.365	0.367	0.367	0.366	0.367	0.371	0.371
One Coat									
Flat 1	0.365	0.367	0.367	0.364	0.370	0.370	0.371	0.373	0.373
Flat 2	0.356	0.356	0.365	0.365	0.365	0.365	0.3685	0.367	0.361
Flat 3	0.361	0.365	0.367	0.368	0.3685	0.367	0.369	0.372	0.3715
Two Coats									
Flat 1	0.367	0.3695	0.370	0.367	0.372	0.373	0.373	0.375	0.375
Flat 2	0.3585	0.359	0.368	0.367	0.3675	0.368	0.371	0.369	0.3625
Flat 3	0.363	0.368	0.369	0.3705	0.3705	0.370	0.3715	0.375	0.374

Fig. 51: Varnish thickness measurements.

Result: Average varnish thickness for two coats when measured across the flats of a rod as when measuring a taper amounts to 0.0037". This number would have to be adjusted upwards if more coats were used or if the coats were thicker, and downward if thinner or fewer coats were used.

Effect of Glue Thickness on Rod Size

Many builders have spent hours planing their cane strips to an exact size so as to produce a particular taper in the final product only to find that the rod was oversized after it was glued up. The cause of this phenomenon is the change brought about by the thickness of the glue. This can vary depending on the type of glue and the binding pressure, but in most of the rods built by the author, the glue thickness turned out to be about 0.001". The effect of this layer between the splines is calculated as increasing the overall rod thickness "d" across the flats on a hex rod by 0.005". The mathematics for this calculation is shown in Fig. 52.

Fig. 52: Hex rod thickness gain due to 0.001" glue.

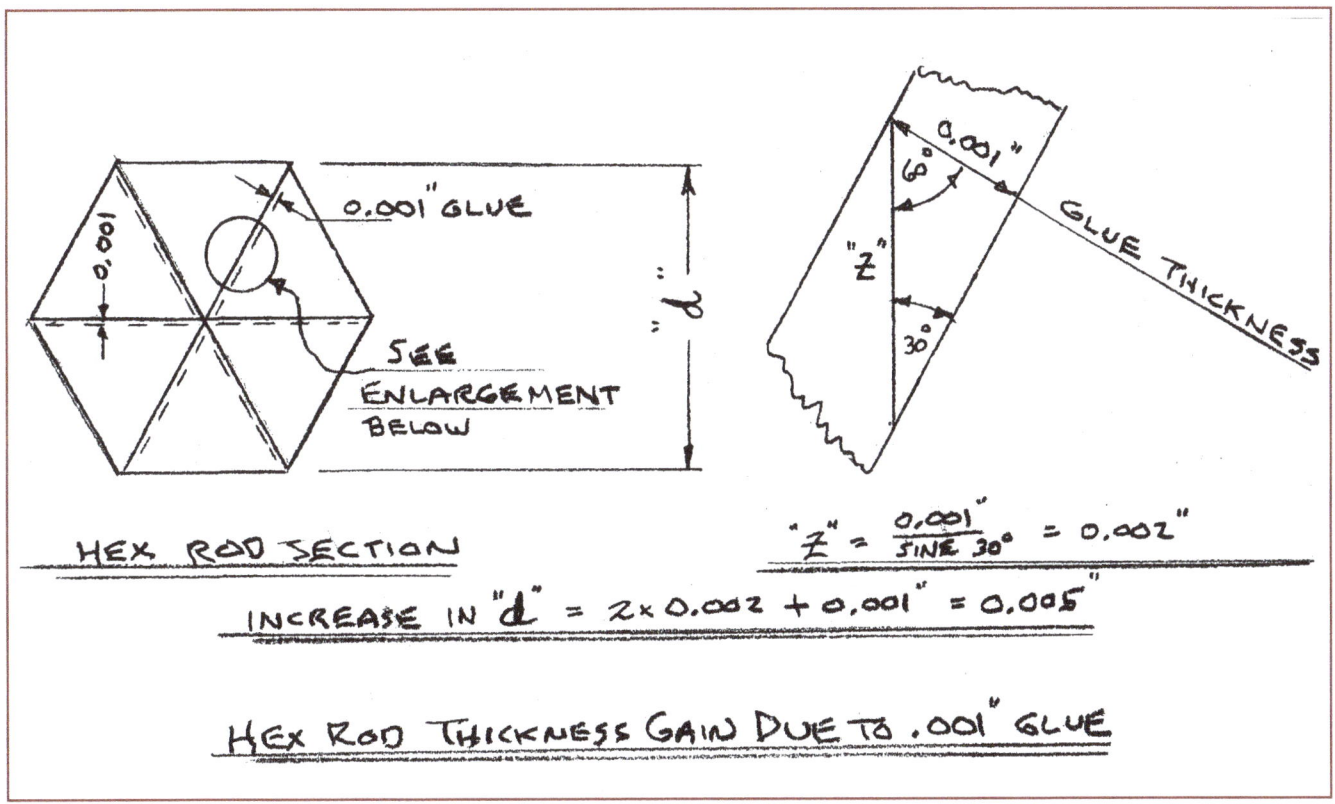

TIP No. 12: FINISHING AND GLUING   33

Tip No. 13
Nodeless Rods

These procedures regarding nodeless rod-making have been furnished by fellow rod-builder and fishing partner Jack Byrd of Edmonds, Washington. He has considerable experience in this particular field and offers many helpful ideas.

Dealing with the nodes in building bamboo fly rods is a bothersome task. Nodes are reputed to form positions of weakness, hard and sometimes irregular spots. They must be straightened and smoothed out to match the adjacent areas of the cane. It is also common practice to stagger the nodes in some predetermined pattern among the splines in a rod section. Since the nodes are a bother, getting rid of them seems a logical conclusion and although significant work is involved it may be worthwhile.

The only extra tools required for nodeless construction are a scarfing jig and some clamps. The scarfing block is a simple device made from two short rectangular blocks of hard wood or metal with an angled plate inserted and fastened between them. The easiest type to build is made from two matched blocks of hardwood about 8" x 1" x 3/4". A piece of wood or plastic 1/8"-thick x 1" x 8"-long with a 3-4"-long bevel of 4° cut from one surface is inserted between the blocks such that the flat top and bottom surfaces of all three pieces are flush. The three pieces are then pinned together using nails or screws in drilled holes in such a way that it can be easily opened to receive a strip or "splint" of bamboo to be scarfed. The device is then closed tightly in a vise to hold the "splint" at the 4° for planing. A better version of this jig, made from steel pieces, is shown in Fig. 53 and Fig. 54.

Fig. 53: Scarfing block parts.

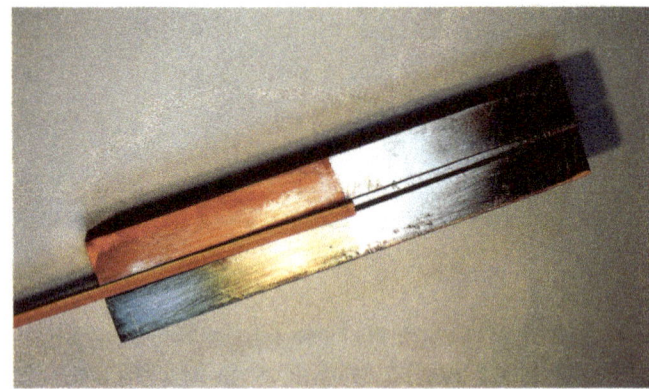

Fig. 54: Scarfing block assembled with cane piece to be planed.

The improved version has a center bevel plate having a 4"-long by 5° bevel on one side and a 3"-long by 3 1/2° bevel on the other side to provide the builder with two options. The jig is aligned by two 3/16" diameter pins and held together with three (3) no.10-32 screws, two of which are spring loaded.

Procedure

The following steps are used to make a nodeless spline:

1. Select a culm of bamboo. Using one that has nodes spaced farther apart will of course result in fewer splices.

2. Cut out the nodes. Cut through the whole diameter of the culm if you wish. Make the cuts far enough from the center of the nodes that the area of straight fibers has been reached. This will be about 1" from the center of the node. Use a fine-toothed hack saw, a band saw or a fine-toothed Japanese razor saw. Mark the butt end of each (now nodeless) piece with a colored pen for registration and further reference. The original order of the pieces in the culm will be obvious because of their graduated lengths. Most rod makers heat-treat at this point, using their kitchen oven.

3. Split the bamboo pieces into "splints" of sufficient width to make the splines for the rod plus an allowance for dressing the splints to have sides 90° to the rind. This is necessary so that they will fit properly in the bottom of the scarfing block.

4. Determine the order of the splints used to form the appropriate length needed for the rod splines. The longer distances between the former node positions toward the tip of the culm makes these splints the most desirable, providing they are thick enough (fewer scarfs to be made). It is not necessary that all splints be used in the original order from the culm. Remember to allow for the shortening caused by making the scarfed joints. In a three-piece nodeless rod example, a five-splint butt section spline made from 50" of pre-scarfed splints resulted in a 34" spline.

5. Plane off the pith side of the splint so that it is approximately parallel to the enamel (rind) side. Then plane off the sides of the splint so they are flat (90° to the pith and rind sides), thus forming a generally rectangular cross section.

6. Place a prepared splint in the sufficiently opened scarfing block so that the bottom edge of the tip of the spint extends a little beyond the point where the bevel plate meets the surface of the side bars. Press the spint down firmly against the angle plate. Mount the scarfing block in a vise and clamp it firmly against the splint. Now plane off all of the bamboo that extends up above the the flat surface of the scarfing block until it is exactly flush. Final removal of the bamboo to bring it flush may be done with a file or sanding block. Note which side of the block is faced by the rind (enamel) of the bamboo. Scarf joints are designated "left" or "right". In keeping with this, the splints are marked accordingly. Note here that Jack uses his sea-going background coloring the bars on his scarfing blocks green for right or starboard, and red for left or port as shown in the photos. Next repeat the clamping and planing steps for the next splint to be mated with the first. Be sure the rind is on the same side as that of the first splint. Normal practice is for adjacent splines to be planed on opposite sides. Thus in a given rod section splines 1, 3, 5 are "right" scarfed while splines 2, 4, 6 are "left " scarfed.

7. When all of the splints necessary for a rod section have been planed to the scarfing angle, the next step is assembly. Scarfs to be mated are first placed and then held in position with one or more small spring clamps. The order of assembly should be coded to ensure the correct order is maintained. Some makers use a color code. Jack marks his splints with a pencil coding "1T1R" for the first spline of the tip section, first scarf, right bevel; next will be "1T2R" for the first spline of the tip section, 2nd scarf, right bevel; etc. The mating surfaces should be dry-fitted together, aligned for straightness and witness marked with a pencil for the gluing fit.

8. Glue is spread on the beveled surfaces to be mated and pressed together, matching up the witness marks and the enameled surfaces. This must be done very carefully and exactly so that the surfaces are smooth, level and flush. The best way to do this is to run your fingers over the splice to see there is no offset. Next, the splints are firmly clamped together to hold them until the glue hardens. Three small spring clamps are needed at each scarfed joint.

9. When the glue is hard and dry, the clamps are removed and the glue joints dressed. First the excess glue is cleaned from the enamel side by carefully scraping or filing. A smooth surface should result. Next the pith side of all joints, the whole length of the strip, is planed flat. Now the sides of the joints are planed in the direction of the scarfs until all are smooth and flat. The strips are now ready to be made into tapered splines with triangular cross sections by regular rod-making methods.

10. Here are some special matters to be considered with respect to nodeless construction:

- At present, no one seems to have found the perfect glue to use. Titebond and Titebond II are clean to use and set up rapidly, but suffer from failure if heated.
- Hot Stuff–Super T set up far too quickly for proper alignment.
- Resorcinal leaves a maroon glue line.
- Jack has settled on a thinned URAC 185 which is slow setting and messy but strong and heat resistant, and the same adhesive used to glue the splines together.
- Significant work is involved in making nodeless rods although some claim it is actually faster.
- It is probably better to stagger the scarfs in the splines of a rod section rather than having them lined up in a picket fence pattern.

Tip No. 14
Quadrate Rods and Tapers

Making 4-sided rods is not as easy as it may seem at first glance. One reason for this is that the final planing form must have a left-hand and a right-hand tapered groove. Another is that it's a bit more difficult to measure the form depth needed to make a certain-sized strip. A roughing form for producing non-tapered strips cut oversize is shown in Fig. 55. This form can be made from maple, as is shown, or from steel. Note that left- and right-hand grooves are not required in this form since the strips are not yet tapered from end to end. The push-pull screws allow the strip size to be varied to suit the rod being produced.

Fig. 55: Quadrate roughing form for quadrate rods.

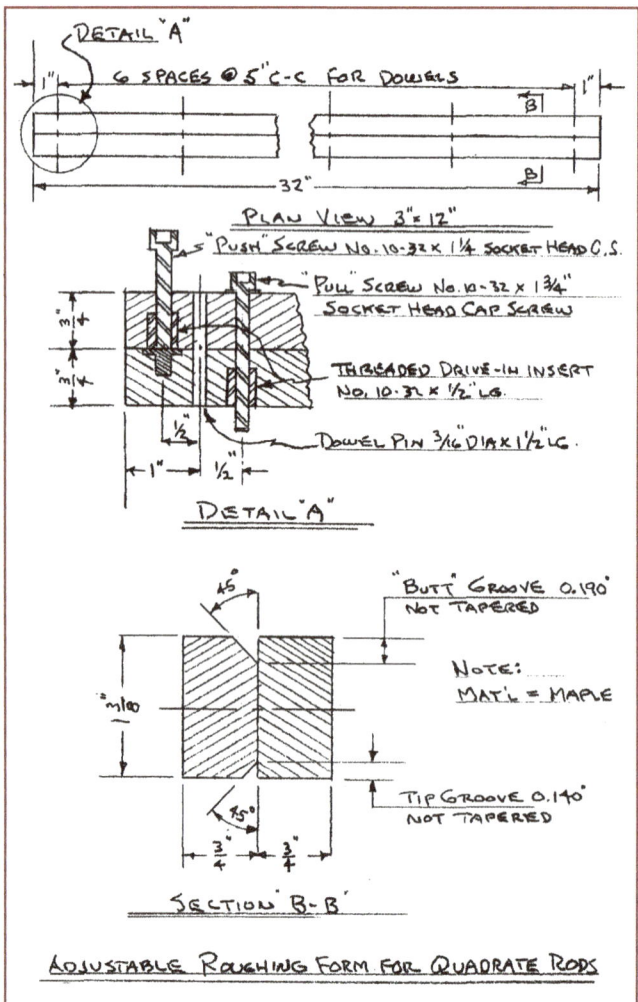

Once the roughed-out strips are prepared the next step will be to put the taper in each of the four strips. A drawing of a 62"-long push-pull final planing bar is shown in Fig. 56.

Note that the bar consists of three separate pieces aligned with steel dowel pins and adjusted every five inches with push-pull screws. Various materials may be used for the planing bars. In the model shown, the center section is maple and the two outer bars are ultra-high molecular weight polyethylene. In constructing this form it is recommended that the top and bottom surfaces be finished after the bar is assembled so that all the surfaces are flush with each other. A photograph of a planing bar constructed of polyethylene and maple is shown in Fig. 57.

Fig. 57: Final planing bar.

The trick in making this form is in cutting the tapered grooves in the center section. To do this task, the center section was mounted on top of a master shim two inches wide and sixty-two inches long which itself was tapered 0.018"/ft over its entire length. The tapered angles are then cut using a 45° router bit passed horizontally along the length of the strip. A drawing of the master shim is shown in Fig. 58.

36 ● CANE RODS: TIPS & TAPERS

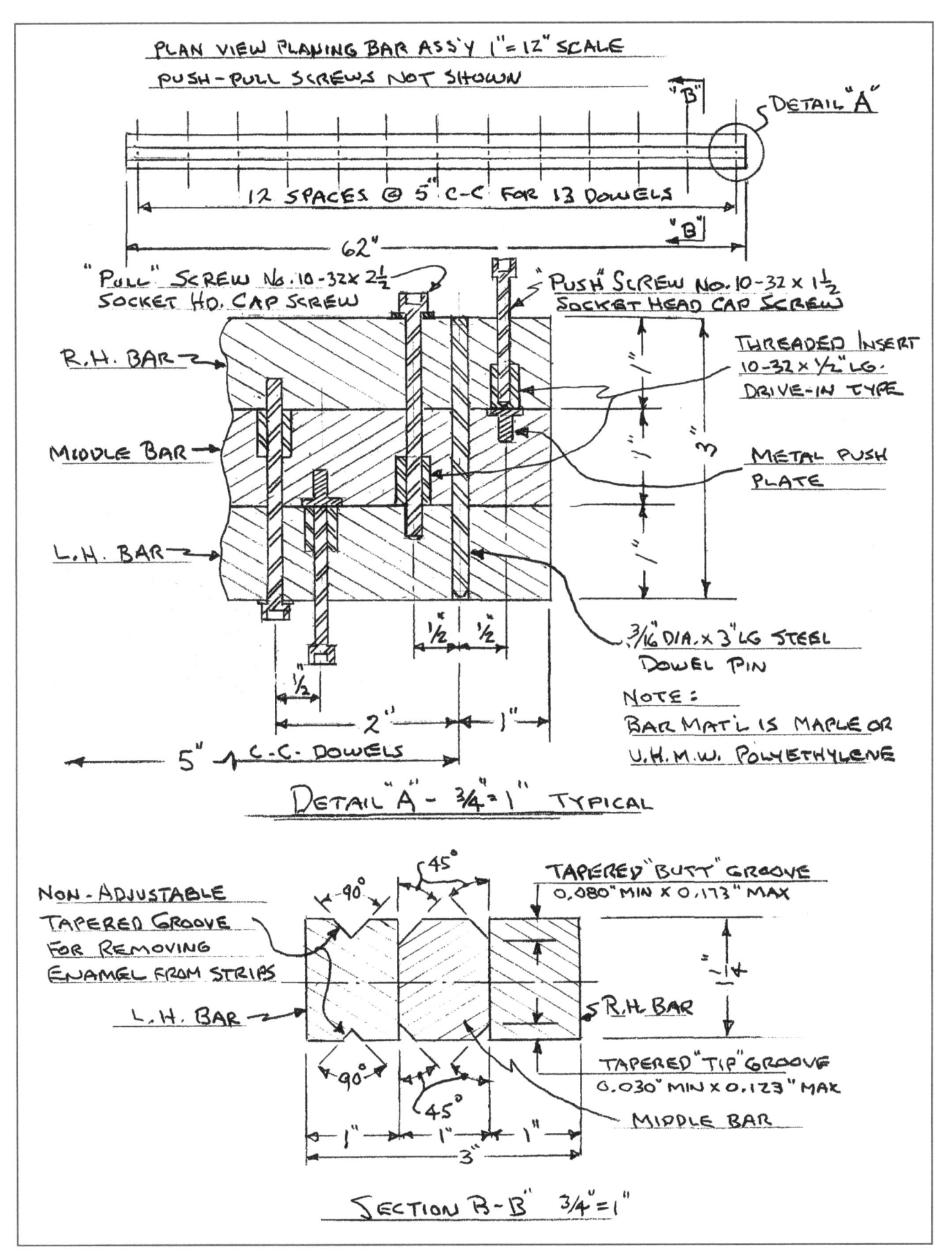

Fig. 56: Final planing bar for a quadrate rod.

Tip No. 14: Quadrate Rods and Tapers

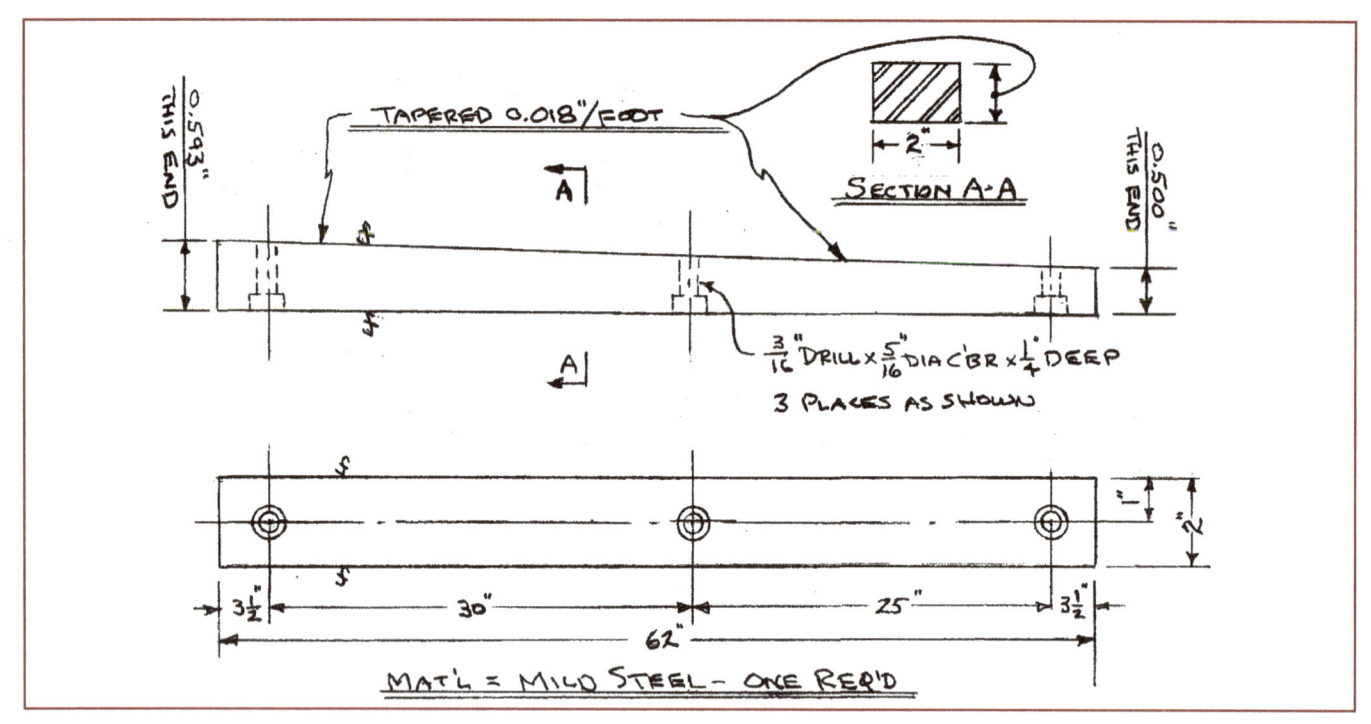

Fig. 58: Master shim for cutting the tapered grooves.

After the strips have had the tapered grooves cut in them, the final operation is to flatten off the enamel side of each strip. To do this, the four strips are placed one at a time in the 90° tapered groove provided for this purpose in the planing form. Just kiss the enamel by sanding, being careful not to remove the power fibers beneath. Visual inspection will reveal when the enamel has been removed. Assembling quadrates is different from usual in that the ferrule(s) need to fit a four-sided rod rather than a six-sided rod. There are several steps required to prepare the ferrule. First, it is best to obtain a non-serrated ferrule. Second, the proper-size ferrule must be chosen. A chart is shown in Fig. 59 to aid the builder in the selection.

The third step is to thin down the open end of the ferrule for a distance of about 5/16". Do this carefully using a bench grinder equipped with a fine-grained stone, and finish polishing this surface with a fine file or fine emery paper (at least 600 grit). Then the ferrule must be v-grooved in four (4) places 90° apart. This can be accomplished quite easily using a Dremel grinder equipped with a #7120 diamond bit (same as shown in Tip No. 7). The next step is to square up the bore of the ferrule for about 1/3 of its length starting at the open end. Make a square steel bar 3-4"-long having the same thickness as the size of the rod at the ferrule station. Push the tool gently into the ferrule bore and press the sides square. This can be done by hand, with a vise or with a 4-jawed chuck. Be sure that the squaring tool is not inserted into the ferrule bore too far, stop just short of the water seal inside the ferrule. Also take care that this operation does not distort the cylindrical bore of the female-to-male ferrule fit.

The ferrule may then be blued if so desired and it will be ready for installation. During the assembly, place the v-notches at the corners of the rod and fit the ferrule tightly to the rod. Glue the ferrule in place using U-Bond adhesive, wipe off any excess and bind the tabs tightly with string while the glue dries. After the glue has dried, remove the string carefully so as not to loosen the ferrule tabs. These tabs will then be bound in place with the thread during the guide installation and wrapping operation.

Listed below in Fig. 61 are tapers for a number of 4-sided rods. The Edwards 8'-0" x 2-pc #40 model (owned by Richard Colo) is a particular favorite of mine in the way the rod feels and handles. Edwards made high-quality quadrates and is indeed famous for them.

Fig. 60: Gould's quadrate rod RR-132-8.

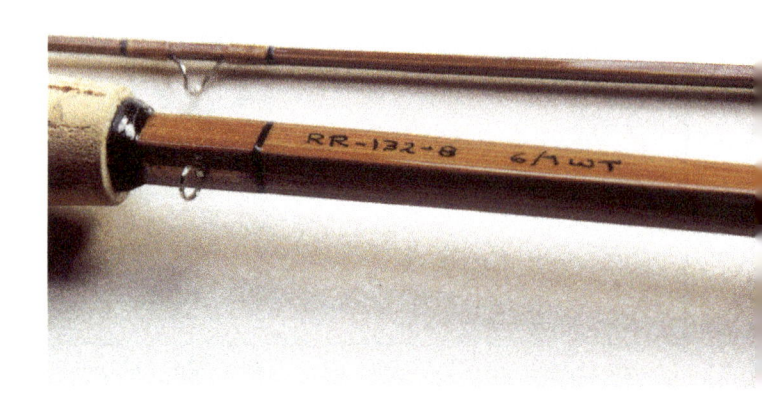

Maker	Edwards	Edwards	Edwards	Edwards	Edwards	Edwards	Gould RR-120-8	Gould
Model	#53-6510	#25	#25	#40	#50		Chironomid	RR-132-8
Length	8'-6" x 3pc.	7'-0" x 2pc.	9'-0" x 3pc.	8'-0"	8'-0"	8'-0" x 3pc.	8'-0" x 2pc.	8'-0" x 2 pc.
Line Size	6wt	4wt			DT5wt	3wt	4/5wt	5/6wt
Station							Soft Action	Soft Action
	"d"	"d"	"d"	"d"	"d"	"d"	"d"	"d"
0	0.07	0.062	0.075	0.062	0.065	0.065	0.06	0.075
5	0.096	0.088	0.093	0.079	0.084	0.081	0.077	0.086
10	0.112	0.103	0.126	0.11	0.102	0.102	0.095	0.091
15	0.13	0.108	0.133	0.122	0.119	0.115	0.109	0.117
20	0.142	0.129	0.137	0.167	0.155	0.14	0.139	0.136
25	0.155	0.137	0.167	0.155	0.14	0.139	0.136	0.138
30	0.166	0.144	0.171	0.163	0.15	0.141	0.148	0.146
35	0.176	0.158	0.182	0.175	0.167	0.155	0.159	0.156
40	0.192	0.158	0.191	0.19	0.185	0.175	0.171	0.162
45	0.194	0.17	0.207	0.202	0.189	0.192	0.182	0.177
50	0.208	0.194	0.222	0.216	0.2	0.208	0.196	0.195
55	0.206	0.202	0.24	0.23	0.207	0.221	0.211	0.196
60	0.224	0.208	0.255	0.242	0.23	0.227	0.228	0.216
65	0.226	0.229	0.267	0.258	0.232	0.244	0.251	0.245
70	0.28	0.239	0.267	0.271	0.242	0.261	0.277	0.263
75	0.29	0.28	0.258	0.287	0.253	0.278	0.31	0.298
80	0.326	grip	0.279	0.292	0.271	0.297	0.331	0.316
85	0.328	grip	0.293	0.34	0.329	0.397	0.342	0.329
90	0.356		0.31				0.348	0.337
95	0.375		0.359				0.349	0.347
100			0.43				0.349	
105			0.43					
110			0.43					

Fig. 61: Quadrate tapers.

Minimum "d" across flats of quad	Maximum "d" across flats of quad	Ferrule size	Ferrule bore	Ferrule bore circumference
0.124"	0.134"	11/64"	0.1719"	0.540"
0.135"	0.147"	12/64"	0.1875"	0.589"
0.148"	0.160"	13/64"	0.2031"	0.638"
0.161"	0.172"	14/64"	0.2188"	0.687"
0.173"	0.184"	15/64"	0.2344"	0.736"
0.185"	0.196"	16/64"	0.2500"	0.785"
0.197"	0.209"	17/64"	0.2656"	0.834"
0.210"	0.221"	18/64"	0.2813"	0.884"
0.222"	0.233"	19/64"	0.2969"	0.933"

Fig. 59: Quadrate rod ferrule selection chart.

Tip No. 15
Spiral Rod Making

History
The history of spiral-rod making dates back to 1892 when Fred D. Devine of Utica, New York, obtained his Patent No. 476370 for the process of making such a rod. Since then few rod-builders have made spiral rods. One fairly recent exception, however, was Letcher Lambuth of Seattle, Washington. He chronicled his efforts in a book titled *The Angler's Workshop* published in 1979.

Theory
The theory behind the spiral rod is that because it is twisted it will be stiffer and stronger than the hex rod it started out to be without additional weight. The mathematics for this claim is based on a claim of increased moment of inertia. The engineering formula for deflection of a cantilevered beam (a beam fixed at one end) is $Y = PL^3/3EI$, where Y= defection, P= load, L= length, E= modulus of elasticity, and I= moment of inertia. This means that the larger the moment of inertia, the lower the deflection. In the case of a spiral rod, if one considers an infinitely twisted rod the cross section changes from a hexagon to a circle whose diameter is equal to the distance across the corners of the original hexagon (a circumscribed circle). Take for example a hexagon that is 0.350" across the flats, it will have a moment of inertia "I" = 0.0009 $inches^4$. Now compare that to the circle circumscribing that hexagon which will have a diameter of 0.404". The moment of inertia for that circle will be "I" = 0.0013 $inches^4$ (substantially larger than the hex – about 44% larger). Therefore it seems logical that a twisted rod will be somewhat stiffer than a hexagonal rod depending upon how many times it is twisted.

The Equipment
Here is a list of the materials required to make a spiral rod form:
- 1 aluminum channel 4"x 1 1/2" x 72"
- 7 Lower clamping bars 1/4"x 3/4"x 4" steel bar stock
- 7 Upper clamping bars 1/4"x 3/4"x 2 3/4" steel bar stock
- 16 Adjusting screws no.10-32 x 2" long
- 16 Adjusting screws no.10-32 x 1 1/2" long
- 1 Drill chuck Jacobs 2B with 5/16-24 threaded bore
- 1 Drill chuck Jacobs 33B with 5/16-24 threaded bore
- 2 Threaded steel rods 5/16-24 x 10" long
- 4 5/16 steel washers
- 4 5/16-24 steel hex nuts
- 2 Wood or metal block bored for the 5/16" rods to hold drill chucks
- 2 Fasteners to secure the blocks to the channel

The Process
To make a spiral fly rod from a hexagonal rod, proceed as follows:
- Make a set of finished splines for the desired hex rod.
- Do not glue these but bind them together with string in the rod binder.
- Determine where the guides are to be located. Use enough guides so that the rod will be twisted about two (2) full turns over its entire length.
- Adjust the spiral rod form drill chuck positions so that they match the length of the splines.

Fig. 62: Spiral rod form assembly.

- Drill and tap the form so that a set of clamping bars may be located at each guide location for this particular rod. Note that each lower clamping bar has four (4) adjusting screws. Two screws push the bar up from the bottom and two pull it down from the top. Make one arrangement for the tip section and another for the butt section.
- Install the rod section in the spiral rod form without any of the clamping bars in contact with the rod section.
- Tighten the drill chuck at each end and place tension on the rod section by tightening up the threaded rods on which the drill chucks are mounted. (This tension pulls the rod section straight and true).
- Raise the lower clamping plate at each guide station (by turning its jack screws) until it just kisses the rod section at that location. Be sure the lower clamping bar is level and locked in place. Do this all along the rod section length.
- Remove the rod section, take off the binding string, glue up the rod and bind it again with string.
- Immediately place the section back in the spiral rod form, tighten up the drill chucks again and apply tension to the rod section once again. Check to be certain that the lower clamping bars are just kissing the bottom of the rod section at each guide station.
- Now lock the drill chuck on the small end in place so that it will not rotate (use a nut on each side of the threaded rod on which the drill chuck is mounted).
- Grasp the drill chuck on the large end of the rod and rotate it so that the rod section twists at the first guide station next to the chuck at the small end of the rod. Note that the twist from guide to guide is always 60° but that the twist between the drill chuck and the first guide and between the last guide and the chuck at the big end may only be 30°.
- Install the top clamping plate against the rod section at that location and tighten it down. This will hold the twist at that location firmly while the glue dries.
- Proceed to the next guide and repeat the process twisting the chuck at the big end by 60° between guide stations. Proceed along the rod section until the twisting is completed.
- Allow the clamped-up section to dry for at least three (3) full days (in a warm place). This is done to be certain that the glue is fully cured.
- After the section is removed from the form and the binding thread is removed, again let the rod sections cure for several additional days before mounting the guides. This allows for "reflex", wherein the rod section may untwist just a bit once the tension stresses are removed.
- Finish the rod as normal but be aware that a twisted rod is extremely difficult to straighten, so get it straight in the form.

A photograph of a rod mounted in the spiral-rod form is shown in Fig. 62, with a close-up of one station shown in Fig. 63.

Fig. 63: Close-up of spiral rod station.

Tip No. 16
Short Rod Tapers for Rods 4'4" to 6'10"

Short fly rods, sometimes called Banty rods, are often used for fishing small streams or creeks where a longer fly rod is neither useful nor desired. In some cases, short rods were made especially for display purposes, or for gifts. The "rise" is shown for each of these rods. This term is the slope of the curve when the thickness dimension "d" is plotted against the distance from the tip measurement. In most cases it is calculated by taking the thickness at station 60 and subtracting the thickness at station 10 and then multiplying the result by (2) two. This then gives the "rise" per 100 inches and is used as a comparative standard in judging rod action. The following three tables show a selection of short rods by various builders:

Fig. 67: Gould's Rod RR-135-5.

Fig. 64: Short rod tapers, sheet 1.

Maker	Anderson	Burgess	Cattanach	Constable	Garrison	Gould	Gould	Hardy
Model		The Brook		Wisp		193	RR-133-5	A&F Banty
Length	6-6"	6'-3"	6'-6"	6"-0" x 2pc.	6'-9"	5"-0"x2pc	6'-0" x 2pc	4'-0" x2pc
Line Size	4wt	6wt	3wt	3wt		4/5wt	5wt	
Rise	0.268	0.298	0.27	0.3	0.258	0.344	0.314	0.3
Action	medium	fast	medium	fast	slow	xfast	xfast	fast
	"d"	"d"	"d"	"d"	"d"	"d"	"d"	"d"
0	0.064	0.093	0.61	0.082	0.063	0.075	0.088	0.07
5	0.078	0.102	0.067	0.092	0.07	0.091	0.094	0.088
10	0.096	0.128	0.086	0.109	0.09	0.1	0.11	0.107
15	0.113	0.145	0.101	0.119	0.108	0.11	0.124	0.119
20	0.127	0.155	0.114	0.143	0.12	0.123	0.137	0.133
25	0.14	0.165	0.126	0.145	0.132	0.14	0.155	0.146
30	0.152	0.183	0.138	0.16	0.144	0.16	0.175	0.175
35	0.165	0.19	0.149	0.167	0.158	0.183	0.182	0.182
40	0.177	0.248	0.162	0.191	0.168	0.203	0.186	0.198
45	0.191	0.261	0.178	0.212	0.181	0.221	0.21	0.205
50	0.204	0.268	0.192	0.221	0.193	0.243	0.228	grip
55	0.217	0.273	0.207	0.241	0.206	0.262	0.243	
60	0.23	0.277	0.221	0.259	0.219	0.272	0.267	
65	0.244	0.289	0.236		0.233		0.283	
70	0.259	0.3	0.236		0.247		0.292	
75	0.274	0.3	0.236		0.26		0.298	
80			0.256		0.29			

Maker	Higham	Leonard	Leonard ACM	Leonard 36H/37H	Nunley Mt. Creek	Nunley	Orvis Mitey Mite
Model							
Length	6'-0"	6'-10"	6'-6" x2pc	6'-0" x 2pc	5'-6"	5'-0" x1pc	5'0" - 2pc
Line Size	6/7wt	4/5wt		3wt	4wt	2wt	
Rise	0.312"	0.226"	0.294	0.228	0.312	0.3	0.342
Action	xfast	xslow	fast	xslow	xfast	fast	xfast
Station							
	"d"	"d"	"d"	"d"	"d"	"d"	"d"
0	0.07	0.068	0.04	0.061	0.066	0.06	tip-top
5	0.09	0.091	0.054	0.07	0.072	0.064	0.089
10	0.103	0.108	0.068	0.083	0.094	0.085	0.1
15	0.122	0.124	0.085	0.094	0.108	0.097	0.108
20	0.139	0.141	0.104	0.108	0.126	0.113	0.123
25	0.153	0.151	0.111	0.122	0.14	0.126	0.14
30	0.172	0.155	0.128	0.132	0.156	0.142	0.16
35	0.184	0.169	0.133	0.141	0.166	0.151	0.183
40	0.19	0.192	0.146	0.148	0.176	0.161	0.203
45	0.206	0.203	0.16	0.163	0.19	0.173	0.221
50	0.228	0.212	0.176	0.173	0.224	0.231	0.243
55	0.248	0.217	0.195	0.186	0.24	0.235	grip
60	0.259	0.221	0.215	0.197	0.25	0.235	
65	0.27	0.241	0.225	0.206	0.25		
70	0.276	0.314	0.307	grip	0.25		
75	0.288	0.349	grip				
80		0.36					

Fig. 65: Short rod tapers, sheet 2.

Maker	Orvis Superfine	Orvis Battenkill	Orvis Superfine	Orvis 663	Orvis Flea	Payne
Model						
Length	6'-6"	6'-6"	6'-0" x1pc	6'-6" x 3pc	6'-0"	4'-4" x2pc
Line Size	5/6wt	5/6wt	5wt	5wt		4wt
Rise	0.23	0.238	0.256	0.33	0.224	0.28
Action	xslow	xslow	slow	xfast	xslow	medium
Station						
	"d"	"d"	"d"	"d"	"d"	"d"
0	0.076	0.75	0.074	0.058	0.075	0.076
5	0.094	0.094	0.092	0.072	0.09	0.092
10	0.111	0.111	0.112	0.08	0.102	0.118
15	0.124	0.122	0.122	0.092	0.114	0.124
20	0.133	0.133	0.135	0.118	0.125	0.138
25	0.144	0.141	0.15	0.132	0.137	0.154
30	0.159	0.152	0.156	0.146	0.15	0.168
35	0.164	0.164	0.169	0.165	0.152	0.178
40	0.17	0.18	0.179	0.18	0.163	0.188
45	0.19	0.197	0.192	0.195	0.182	0.202
50	0.194	0.209	0.204	0.21	0.193	0.202
55	0.207	0.218	0.221	0.23	0.202	0.202
60	0.226	0.23	0.24	0.245	0.214	
65	0.231	0.245	0.268	0.27	0.231	
70	0.246	0.262		0.285	0.26	
75	0.261	0.277		0.29		

Fig. 66: Short rod tapers, sheet 3.

Maker	Pizon & Michel	Powell	Thramer	Winston	Young	Young
Model	Midget				Midge	(2nd) Midge
Length	6'-0" x2pc	5'-0" x2pc	4'-4"	6'-0" x 2pc	6'-3"	6'-3"
Line Size	4wt	5wt	4wt	3wt	4wt	
Rise	0.258	0.302	0.337	0.254	0.268	0.262
Action	slow	xfast	xfast	slow	medium	m edium
Station	"d"	"d"	"d"	"d"	"d"	"d"
0	0.068	0.075	0.068	0.07	0.063	0.068
5	0.076	0.079	0.084	0.079	0.073	0.077
10	0.085	0.095	0.096	0.092	0.092	0.097
15	0.102	0.116	0.114	0.105	0.108	0.117
20	0.117	0.134	0.128	0.118	0.12	0.125
25	0.126	0.136	0.144	0.132	0.136	0.142
30	0.141	0.15	0.158	0.145	0.146	0.147
35	0.157	0.176	0.176	0.158	0.166	0.171
40	0.166	0.188	0.192	0.17	0.179	0.19
45	0.176	0.2	0.22	0.177	0.198	0.207
50	0.185	0.226	grip	0.19	0.202	0.211
55	0.198	grip	grip	0.203	0.218	0.217
60	0.214	grip		0.29	0.226	0.228
65	0.23			0.233	0.236	0.237
70	Handle			swell	grip	
75				grip	grip	

Fig. 67 : Short rod tapers, sheet 4.

Tip No. 17
Spey Rod Tapers

The term Spey rods as used in this chapter means any of the two-handed rods meant for use in Spey casting. They are generally long rods of 11 to 16 feet, and may be made in several sections.

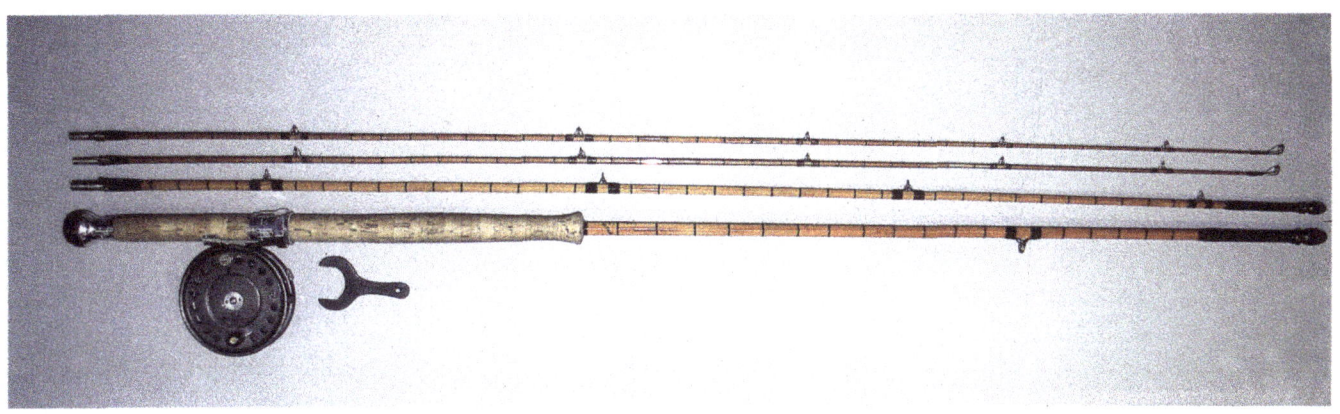

Fig. 69: Hardy Wye Spey rod.

Maker Model	Leonard	Waara	Hoergaard H.C.	Hoergaard Tan	Hoergaard Alta	Gould Rr-155-11 GI	Hardy The Wye
Length	9' x 3pc	12'	12'	13' - 6"	14' x 3pc	11' x3pc	11' x 3pc
Line Size	9wt	6wt	8/9wt	10wt	10wt	7wt	11/12wt
Station	"d"	"d"	"d"	"d"	"d"	"d"	"d"
0	0.112	0.078	0.1	0.1	0.125	0.078	0.107
5	0.131	0.102	0.12	0.12	0.145	0.089	0.122
10	0.149	0.118	0.135	0.15	0.166	0.105	0.147
15	0.171	0.136	0.15	0.17	0.186	0.127	0.165
20	0.184	0.154	0.167	0.202	0.21	0.144	0.178
25	0.206	0.17	0.183	0.215	0.225	0.159	0.189
30	0.218	0.184	0.2	0.228	0.244	0.173	0.202
35	0.237	0.2	0.22	0.237	0.264	0.187	0.213
40	0.246	0.216	0.235	0.253	0.28	0.2	0.226
45	0.267	0.23	0.25	0.27	0.3	0.213	0.237
50	0.279	0.244	0.278	0.286	0.315	0.226	0.247
55	0.286	0.258	0.29	0.3	0.32	0.239	0.282
60	0.28	0.272	0.305	0.332	0.355	0.252	0.293
65	0.284	0.286	0.325	0.352	0.38	0.266	0.309
70	0.306	0.3	0.333	0.375	0.398	0.279	0.318
75	0.319	0.312	0.345	0.391	0.41	0.292	0.33
80	0.332	0.324	0.36	0.409	0.43	0.306	0.341
85	0.338		0.373	0.425	0.445	0.319	0.359
90	0.358	0.348	0.387	0.442	0.46	0.333	0.376
95	0.38	0.358	0.403	0.458	0.477	0.347	0.392
100	0.402	0.378	0.438	0.472	0.5	0.361	0.399
105	0.426	0.388	0.461	0.496	0.524	0.376	0.415
110	0.437	0.398	0.48	0.51	0.543	0.39	0.423
115	0.447	0.41	0.499	0.547	0.555	0.405	handle
120	0.457	0.422	0.515	0.564	0.567	0.419	handle
125	0.482	0.43	0.53	0.583	0.58	0.433	handle
130	0.5	0.43	0.552	0.6	0.597	0.448	handle
135	0.512	0.43	0.57	0.617	0.615	0.454	handle
140	0.522	0.43	0.59		0.633		
145	0.581	0.43	0.6				
150	0.6						
155	0.62						
160	0.625						
165	0.625						
170	0.625						

Fig. 70: Spey rod tapers.

Tip No. 18
Spinning Rod and Casting Rod Tapers

This set of spinning rod and casting rod tapers includes both one-piece and two-piece cane rods. Note too that they vary from short lightweight rods to longer steelhead-type rods.

Fig. 71: Spinning and casting rod tapers, sheet 1.

Maker Model Length Station	Anderson Spinning 6'-0" "d"	Heddon #1650 Stlhd 8'-6" x 2pc Casting Rod "d"	Heddon #850 6'-0" x 1pc Bait Caster "d"	Heddon 851 L 5'-6" x 1pc Bait Caster "d"	Herters 5'-6" Casting Rod "d"	Orvis Superlight 6'-6" x 2pc Spinning "d"	Pizon & Michel Luxor Classic 7'-3" Spinning Rod "d"
0	0.078	0.117	0.11	0.11	0.13	0.087	0.116
5	0.09	0.133	0.12	0.124	0.134	0.1	0.125
10	0.103	0.156	0.13	0.142	0.158	0.117	0.14
15	0.117	0.18	0.144	0.162	0.185	0.124	0.157
20	0.132	0.201	0.162	0.178	0.212	0.137	0.177
25	0.148	0.225	0.182	0.196	0.237	0.147	0.195
30	0.165	0.243	0.198	0.214	0.267	0.158	0.216
35	0.184	0.271	0.208	0.232	0.293	0.171	0.226
40	0.204	0.295	0.228	0.248	0.31	ferrule	0.247
45	0.225	0.318	0.24	0.264	0.328	0.217	0.263
50	0.246	0.344	0.274	0.286	0.36	0.233	0.28
55	0.267	0.361	swell	0.296	0.374	0.251	0.295
60	0.288	0.392			0.374	0.266	0.307
65	0.308	0.427			0.374	0.286	0.323
70	0.33	0.461				Cork grip	Handle
75		0.491				Cork grip	Handle
80		Grip & Seat					Handle
85		Grip & Seat					Handle
90		Grip & Seat					
95		Grip & Seat					
100		Grip & Seat					
105		Grip & Seat					

Maker	South bend	P.H. Young	P.H. Young	P.H. Young	P.H. Young
Model	634-5	Spinmaster	Spincaster	Special	Exp. Stlhd
Length	5'-0" x 1pc	7'-2" x 2pc	6'-3" x 2pc	6'-4" x 2pc	8'-9" x 2pc
Station	Bait Caster				
	"d"	"d"	"d"	"d"	"d"
0	0.106	0.082	0.096	0.098	0.132
5	0.116	0.091	0.098	0.101	0.14
10	0.118	0.106	0.115	0.122	0.158
15	0.135	0.126	0.142	0.148	0.188
20	0.142	0.143	0.158	0.158	0.214
25	0.147	0.157	0.174	0.17	0.232
30	0.216	0.176	0.191	0.194	0.245
35	0.22	0.192	0.219	0.224	0.26
40	0.243	0.207	0.216	0.226	0.268
45	0.308	0.208	0.224	0.238	0.276
50	0.351	0.211	0.241	0.24	0.298
55	handle	0.216	0.25	0.257	ferrule
60		0.226	0.266	0.268	0.325
65		0.246	0.274	0.285	0.336
70		0.255			0.342
75		0.259			0.363
80					0.38
85					0.403

Fig. 72: Spinning and casting rod tapers, sheet 2.

Fig. 73: Pizon and Michel spinning rod.

Tip No. 19
Pentagonal Rods

ive-sided pentagonal rods are somewhat unusual and not too often seen. This rod design stirs up controversy as to whether or not it is superior to hexagonal and quadrate rods due to the unique geometry of its cross section. The theory often advanced is that the design is inherently stiffer because the guides are placed on one flat that is opposite a peak or strong point on the other side. An analysis of the design properties of various cross sections of equal areas comparing moments of inertia shows that the pentagonal cross section is very slightly stiffer than a hexagon and slightly less stiff than a square.

The major concern in making pentagonal rods is that they are more difficult and more expensive. The planing form for making the five strips must have two (2) grooves, a left hand and a right hand, and thus is more difficult and expensive to make, especially for the home workshop. Then the measuring of the strip size while it is being planed becomes much more complicated.

To convert the taper of a hexagonal rod to a pentagonal rod multiply the distance across the flats "d" of the hex rod by 0.574 to get dimension "R_2" which is the depth measured in the pentagonal form. This will produce a pentagonal rod that has a cross-sectional area equal to that of the hexagonal rod.

If you measure a pentagonal rod and wish to reproduce it, measure the peak to flat dimension "A" of the pentagonal

Fig. 74: Position of strip in pentagonal planing form.

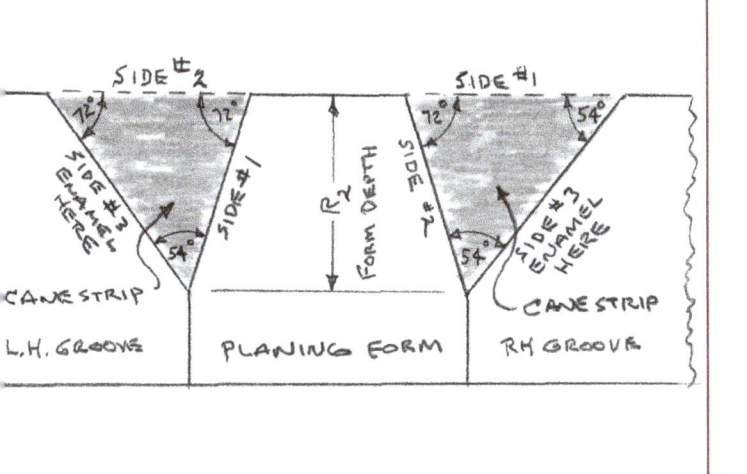

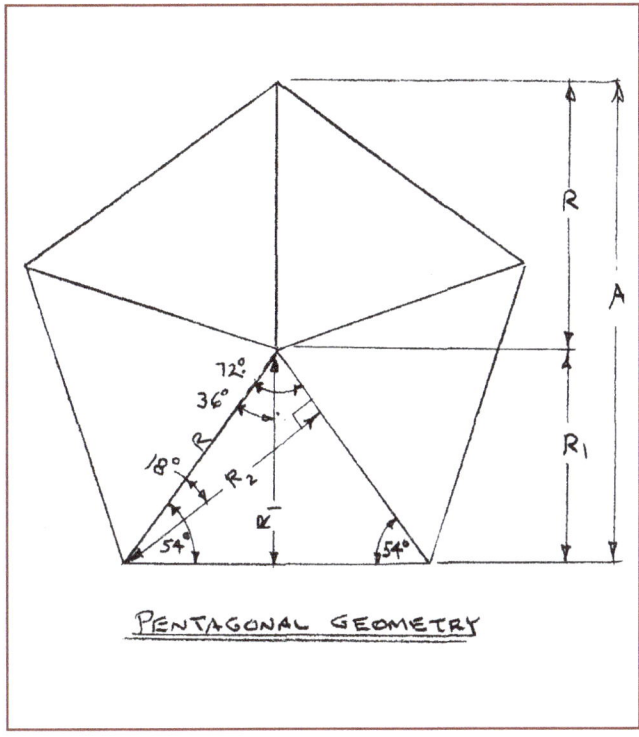

Fig. 77: Pentagonal geometry.

rod and divide it by 1.903 to get the "R_2" dimension. Again, this is the depth measured in the pentagonal form when making the strips. See the sketches below:

Pentagonal Rod Tapers
The tapers shown here for five-sided rods are by Nat Uslan and Harry Faggetter of Spokane, Washington with conversions to 5" stations by R. J. Gould.

Pentagon Cross Section
Figure 77 shows cross section of a pentagon and the definition of the various dimensions.

Derivation of the Dimensions:
$A = R + R_1$, $R = R_1 / \cosine 36$ degrees $= 1.236 R_1$
$R_2 = \cosine 18$ degrees $\times R = 0.951 R = 0.951 \times 1.236 R_1$
$R_1 = R_2 / 1.175$
$R = R_2 / 0.951$
$A = R_1 + R_2 = R_2 / 0.951 + R_2 / 1.175 = 1.903 R_2$
$R_2 = A / 1.903$

Station	Garrison Pentagonal 212E 8ft x 2pc by Faggetter Form depth R2	Kreider Pentagonal 7'-6" by Faggetter Form depth R2	McClane Pentagonal 8'-0" by Faggeter Form depth R2	Uslan Spencer 9016 Pentagonal 9'-0" x 2pc Form depth R2
0	0.043	0.031	0.034	0.044
5	0.049	0.04	0.042	0.051
10	0.061	0.047	0.05	0.057
15	0.071	0.055	0.06	0.066
20	0.079	0.065	0.067	0.076
25	0.087	0.075	0.073	0.085
30	0.095	0.082	0.08	0.095
35	0.102	0.087	0.088	0.103
40	0.109	0.093	0.095	0.107
45	0.116	0.1	0.103	0.115
50	0.123	0.106	0.109	0.12
55	0.131	0.114	0.116	0.123
60	0.138	0.123	0.123	0.125
65	0.146	0.127	0.132	0.133
70	0.153	0.132	0.14	0.144
75	0.161	0.137	0.147	0.151
80	0.17	0.14	0.156	0.159
85	0.189	0.142	0.161	0.167
90	0.195	0.143	0.161	0.171
95	0.195		0.161	0.171
100				handle
105				handle

Fig. 75: Pentagonal rod tapers.

Point to Flat Dimension "A" on a pentagonal rod Minimum	Point to Flat Dimension "A" on a pentagonal rod Maximum	Use ferrule size
0.176	0.192	11/64
0.193	0.210	12/64
0.211	0.227	13/64
0.228	0.245	14/64
0.246	0.262	15/64
0.263	0.280	16/64
0.281	0.297	17/64
0.298	0.314	18/64

Fig. 76: Ferrule selection chart for pentagonal rods.

Tip No. 20
Taper Collection

This set of bamboo rod tapers has been accumulated over many years of rod building. The source for these tapers is from personal measurements, books, periodicals such as the planning form, workshops and from other rod builders. They are listed in alphabetical order by the maker's name.

How to Measure the Taper of a Rod

Each of these tapers is shown for a bare rod with *no varnish*. If the rod is impregnated, the taper is shown over the impregnation. The dimension system used is the standard 5" incremental spacing starting at the tip top with the rod assembled. Where it is known, the line size is shown.

What is Meant By the Term "Rise"

In some cases the "rise" is shown. This term means the slope of the curve when the thickness dimension "d" (distance across the flats of a hex or quadrate rod in inches) is plotted against the distance from the tip in inches. The rise is measured at station 10" and subtracted from station 60" then multiplied by 2 to give the equivalent for the rise of 100". The steepness of this curve is an indication of the stiffness of the rod and allows the builder to compare rod action designs. A guide to rod actions for various "rises" is as follows:

Taper design allowances

When designing a rod taper, several special factors should be taken into account. First is the thickness of the first 5" of the tip section. This part of the rod is subject to very high stresses and is also the thinnest part of the rod. Then, too, the amount of power fibers in the area is very limited. To prevent breakage in this area it is wise to beef up the taper in the first 5" somewhat above the theoretical stress design curve data. This can be accomplished by having little taper in the first 5" below the 5" thickness dimension. A plot of this idea is shown on page 272 in Garrison's book *A Master's Guide to Building a Bamboo Fly Rod*.

Secondly, it may be desirable to flatten out the taper just a bit for a short area where a ferrule is located. By doing this, the extra stiffness provided by the metal ferrule is offset and the thickness of the cane where both the male and female ferrules are mounted will be more nearly the same.

Third, the type of rod action desired can be factored into the design by adjusting the "rise" of the curve obtained when plotting rod thickness versus distance from the tip. Refer to the chart above.

Fourth, The type of stress curve desired can also be incorporated into the taper design. For example if parabolic stresses are used in the taper-design calculations the rod will have a thinner butt section than one designed with straight line stresses. This type of rod will flex more in the lower butt section and handle portion of the rod and is preferred by some.

Fig. 78: Montague splitswitch in "form" case.

Taper Collection: Anderson

Maker	Anderson, Don	Anderson, Don	Anderson, Don	Anderson, Don
Model	Dainty		Spinning Rod	Favorite
Length	6'-0"	6'-6"	6'-0"	7'-9"
Line Size	2wt	4wt		5wt
Station	"d"	"d"	"d"	"d"
0	0.06	0.064	0.078	0.064
5	0.069	0.078	0.09	0.078
10	0.089	0.096	0.103	0.1
15	0.104	0.113	0.117	0.117
20	0.114	0.127	0.132	0.131
25	0.126	0.14	0.148	0.144
30	0.14	0.152	0.165	0.156
35	0.158	0.165	0.184	0.168
40	0.17	0.177	0.204	0.181
45	0.182	0.191	0.225	0.194
50	0.196	0.204	0.246	0.206
55	0.211	0.217	0.267	0.22
60	0.225	0.23	0.288	0.233
65	0.239	0.244	0.308	0.247
70	0.253	0.259	0.33	0.26
75		0.274		0.275
80				0.289
85				0.303
90				0.318
95				0.318

Taper Collection: Bogart to Burgess

Maker	Bogart, Chris	Bogart, Chris	Bokstrom	Bokstrom	Bokstrom	Bramton, W.	Burgess & Ely
Model	Big Dog	Yellow Rose	Med-slow	Medium	Medium	salmon 3pc	The Brook
Length	9 1/2ft x 3pc	7'-0" x 2pc	7'-9"	8'-3"	9'-0"	9'-6"	6'-4"
Line Size	8wt	2wt	DT4	DT6	DT8		5wt
Station	"d"	"d"	"d"	"d"	"d"	"d"	"d"
0	0.07	0.062	0.062	0.074	0.082	0.105	0.08
5	0.084	0.068	0.073	0.091	0.101	0.124	0.105
10	0.104	0.088	0.093	0.114	0.123	0.147	0.122
15	0.128	0.102	0.11	0.133	0.142	0.167	0.139
20	0.144	0.116	0.124	0.146	0.159	0.182	0.151
25	0.158	0.128	0.137	0.16	0.174	0.204	0.163
30	0.172	0.14	0.15	0.172	0.185	0.218	0.178
35	0.186	0.15	0.163	0.184	0.197	0.233	0.186
40	0.2	0.166	0.175	0.197	0.209	0.247	0.211
45	0.218	0.18	0.188	0.209	0.221	0.254	0.261
50	0.234	0.188	0.201	0.22	0.233	0.264	0.268
55	0.248	0.204	0.214	0.232	0.244	0.275	0.273
60	0.266	0.212	0.227	0.244	0.256	0.279	0.277
65	0.278	0.23	0.24	0.255	0.269	0.3	0.289
70	0.286	0.255	0.253	0.267	0.281	0.322	0.3
75	0.296	0.28	0.267	0.279	0.293	0.341	0.31
80	0.314		0.281	0.292	0.307	0.355	
85	0.332		0.295	0.305	0.32	0.372	
90	0.35		0.309	0.318	0.333	0.379	
95	0.366		0.317	0.33	0.346	0.384	
100	0.376			0.342	0.359	0.388	
105	0.38				0.374	0.398	
110					0.385	0.412	

Taper Collection: Cattanach to Cross

Maker	Cattanach	Cattanach	Clark, Bob	Clark, Bob	Constable	Cortland	Cross
Model			Med. Fast	Slow Action	Wisp	444	Sylph
Length	8'-6"	6'-6"	7'-6"	8'-0"	6'-0"	8'-0" x 2pc	7'-0"
Line Wt	4wt	3wt	7wt	6wt	3wt		7wt
Station	"d"	"d"	"d"	"d"	"d"	"d"	"d"
0	0.075	0.061	0.08	0.079	0.082	0.092	0.062
5	0.083	0.067	0.096	0.091	0.092	0.102	0.091
10	0.098	0.086	0.112	0.11	0.109	0.115	0.108
15	0.113	0.101	0.128	0.125	0.119	0.132	0.12
20	0.127	0.114	0.145	0.143	0.144	0.144	0.137
25	0.141	0.126	0.161	0.157	0.145	0.157	0.153
30	0.156	0.138	0.181	0.162	0.161	0.17	0.168
35	0.169	0.149	0.193	0.169	0.167	0.183	0.187
40	0.187	0.162	0.205	0.181	0.185	0.198	0.2
45	0.202	0.178	0.201	0.187	0.191	0.212	0.22
50	0.211	0.192	0.225	0.204	0.212	0.212	0.237
55	0.218	0.207	0.232	0.217	0.221	0.248	0.25
60	0.229	0.221	0.245	0.235	0.241	0.259	0.26
65	0.239	0.236	0.263	0.247	0.251	0.27	0.272
70	0.245	0.236	0.283	0.26		0.281	0.283
75	0.256	0.236	0.298	0.274		0.292	0.29
80	0.268	0.236	0.313	0.287		0.304	0.29
85	0.279		0.328	0.313		0.318	0.29
90	0.288		0.343	0.315		handle	
95	0.288					handle	

Taper Collection: Dam & Dickerson

Maker	Dam	Dickerson	Dickerson	Dickerson	Dickerson	Dickerson	Dickerson
Model	Federlicht	801611	7012	7613	8013	8014	8015
Length	2.55 meters	8'-0"	7'-0"	7'-6"	8'-0"	8'-0"	8'-0"
Line Wt				5wt	5wt	5wt	4wt?
Station	"d"	"d"	"d"	"d"	"d"	"d"	"d"
0	0.08	0.071	0.067	0.068	0.074	0.076	0.094
5	0.092	0.085	0.083	0.09	0.082	0.095	0.107
10	0.105	0.106	0.096	0.104	0.095	0.114	0.12
15	0.118	0.124	0.112	0.122	0.115	0.133	0.135
20	0.132	0.138	0.127	0.14	0.129	0.151	0.15
25	0.143	0.151	0.141	0.155	0.145	0.167	0.166
30	0.153	0.157	0.156	0.17	0.16	0.181	0.179
35	0.175	0.194	0.165	0.18	0.17	0.192	0.192
40	0.19	0.199	0.177	0.198	0.18	0.2	0.205
45	0.204	0.215	0.197	.208/.213	0.189	0.208	0.218
50	0.222	0.219	0.204	0.22	0.215	0.223	0.232
55	0.234	0.23	0.213	0.238	0.232	0.243	0.25
60	0.255	0.243	0.229	0.256	0.251	0.264	0.269
65	0.266	0.261	0.242	0.274	0.272	0.284	0.287
70	0.291	0.274	0.255	0.288	0.293	0.295	0.307
75	0.304	0.29	0.307	0.298	0.304	0.315	0.324
80	0.321	0.317	0.323	0.344	0.318	0.336	0.342
85	0.34		0.323	0.36	0.344	0.359	0.357
90	0.353			0.36	0.375	0.36	0.371
95							0.375

Taper Collection: Dickerson & Divine

Maker	Dickerson	Dickerson	Dickerson	Divine	Divine	Divine	Divine
Model	8015	8615	8617	Fairy	Standard		Fairy
Length	8'-0"	8'-6"	8'-6"	7'-6"	7'-0"	7'-0"	6'-8"
Line Size	4wt?	3wt?	6wt	3wt		3wt	3wt
Station	"d"	"d"	"d"	"d"	"d"	"d"	"d"
0	0.094	0.094	0.066	0.067	0.082	0.062	0.05
5	0.107	0.107	0.078	0.079	0.087	0.087	0.07
10	0.12	0.12	0.102	0.095	0.1	0.105	0.084
15	0.135	0.135	0.114	0.109	0.113	0.115	0.109
20	0.15	0.15	0.132	0.115	0.128	0.127	0.118
25	0.166	0.166	0.152	0.124	0.146	0.14	0.132
30	0.179	0.179	0.166	0.146	0.156	0.155	0.14
35	0.192	0.192	0.18	0.163	0.159	0.167	0.153
40	0.205	0.205	0.188	0.171	0.177	0.177	0.16
45	0.218	0.218	0.196	0.182	0.189	0.188	0.178
50	0.232	0.232	0.208	0.191	0.208	0.198	0.188
55	0.25	0.25	0.22	0.2	0.218	0.21	0.202
60	0.269	0.269	0.236	0.217	0.24	0.22	0.214
65	0.287	0.287	0.254	0.238	0.274	0.233	0.226
70	0.307	0.307	0.266	0.251	0.295	0.247	0.244
75	0.324	0.324	0.286	0.262	0.43	0.262	72 = 0.305
80	0.342	0.342	0.298	0.271		0.277	75 = 0.31
85	0.357	0.357	0.308	.		0.3	80 = 0.325
90	0.371	0.371	0.338				
95	0.375	0.375	0.36				

Taper Collection: Edwards

Maker	Edwards	Edwards	Edwards	Edwards	Edwards	Edwards	Edwards
Model	6 strip	#53-6510	Quad #25	Quad #40	Quad #50	Quad #25	6 strip
Length	8'-0"	8'-6" quad	7'-0"	8'-0"	8'-0"	9'-0"	9'-0"
Line Size	3wt	6wt	4DT		DT5		
Station	"d"	"d"	"d"	"d"	"d"	"d"	"d"
0	0.065	0.07	0.062	0.062	0.065	0.075	0.075
5	0.081	0.096	0.088	0.079	0.084	0.093	0.097
10	0.102	0.112	0.103	0.11	0.102	0.126	0.12
15	0.115	0.13	0.108	0.122	0.119	0.133	0.142
20	0.127	0.142	0.129	0.138	0.13	0.137	0.157
25	0.139	0.155	0.137	0.155	0.14	0.167	0.17
30	0.141	0.166	0.144	0.163	0.15	0.171	0.19
35	0.155	0.176	0.158	0.175	0.167	0.182	0.195
40	0.175	0.192	0.158	0.19	0.185	0.191	0.207
45	0.192	0.194	0.17	0.202	0.189	0.207	0.225
50	0.208	0.208	0.194	0.216	0.2	0.222	0.237
55	0.221	0.206	0.202	0.23	0.207	0.24	0.24
60	0.227	0.224	0.208	0.242	0.23	0.255	0.245
65	0.244	0.226	0.229	0.258	0.232	0.267	0.26
70	0.261	0.28	0.239	0.271	0.242	0.267	0.275
75	0.278	0.29	0.28	0.287	0.253	0.258	0.287
80	0.297	0.326	grip	0.292	0.271	0.279	0.3
85	0.397	0.328	seat	0.34	0.329	0.293	0.315
90	grip	0.356		grip		0.31	0.33
95	seat	0.375		grip		0.359	0.355
100				seat		0.43	0.365
105						0.43	
110						0.43	

Taper Collection: Garrison

Maker	Fairfield	Garrison	Garrison	Garrison	Garrison	Garrison	Garrison
Model	ala para15	193	201	201E	202E	204E	206
Length	7'-0"	6'-9"	7'-0"	7'-0"	7'-0"	7'-3"	7'-6"
Line Size	4wt DT						
Station	"d"	"d"	"d"	"d"	"d"	"d"	"d
0	0.066	0.063	0.063	0.063	0.063	0.063	0.063
5	0.08	0.07	0.077	0.079	0.08	0.081	0.078
10	0.1	0.09	0.096	0.099	0.1	0.101	0.1
15	0.116	0.106	0.112	0.114	0.116	0.118	0.117
20	0.133	0.12	0.126	0.128	0.13	0.132	0.131
25	0.148	0.132	0.139	0.141	0.143	0.145	0.144
30	0.165	0.144	0.151	0.153	0.155	0.157	0.156
35	0.184	0.156	0.163	0.165	0.167	0.169	0.168
40	0.201	0.168	0.175	0.177	0.179	0.181	0.181
45	0.214	0.181	0.188	0.19	0.192	0.194	0.194
50	0.225	0.193	0.201	0.203	0.204	0.206	0.206
55	0.232	0.206	0.214	0.215	0.216	0.219	0.22
60	0.24	0.219	0.227	0.228	0.229	0.232	0.233
65	0.25	0.233	0.24	0.241	0.242	0.245	0.247
70	0.261	0.247	0.253	0.254	0.256	0.259	0.26
75	0.273	0.26	0.289	0.282	0.287	0.273	0.275
80	0.289	0.277	0.295	0.29	0.291	0.3	0.306
85	0.298		0.302		0.295	0.307	0.312
90							0.317

Fig. 79: Jack Byrd's reel seat cutting jig.

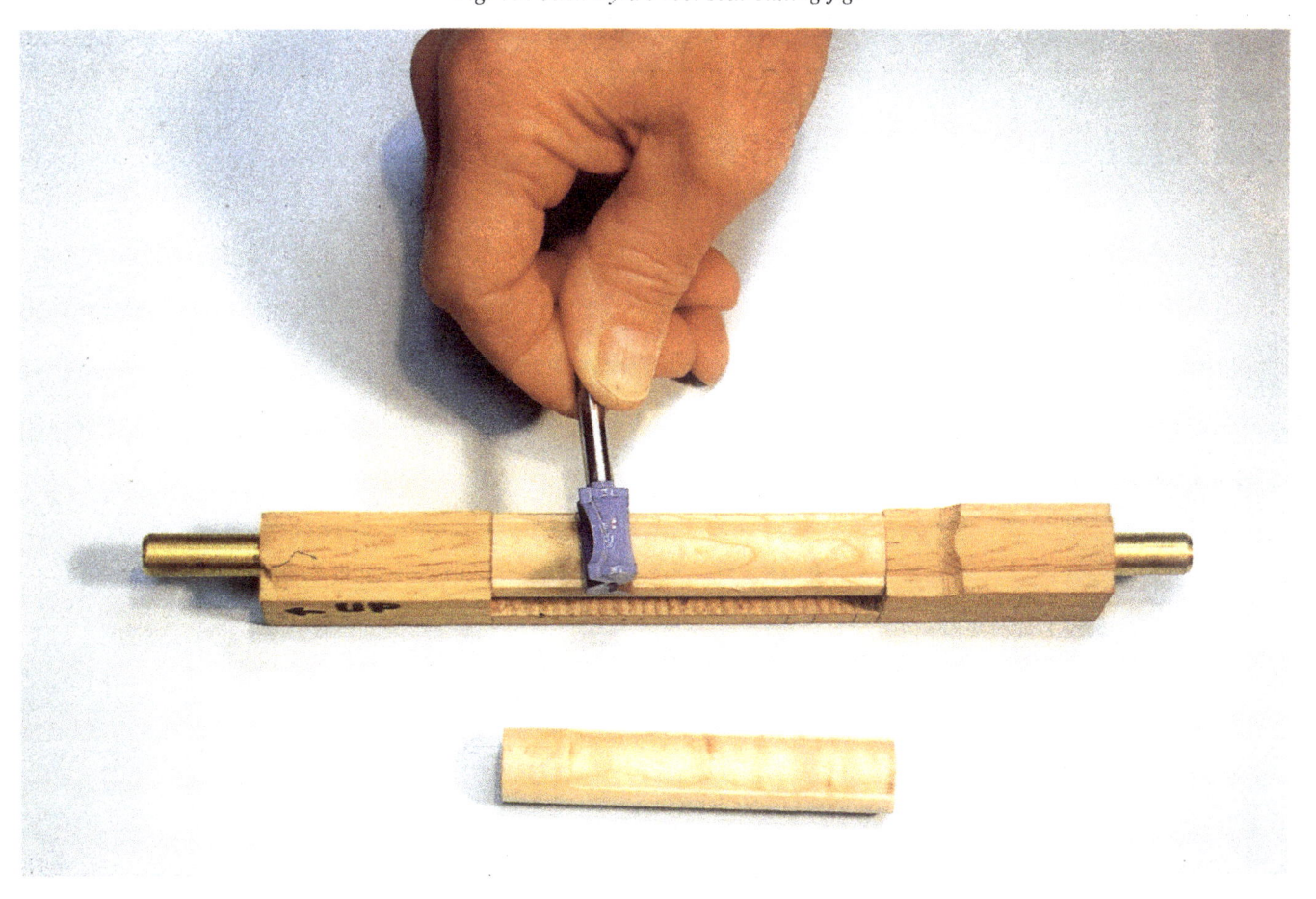

Taper Collection: Garrison

Maker	Garrison	Garrison	Garrison	Garrison	Garrison	Garrison	Garrison
Model	209	209E	212	212E	Pentagonal 212E	215	221
Length	7'-6"	7'-9"	8'-0"	8'-0"	8ft x 2pc	8'-6"x3pc	8'-9"
Line Size							
Station	"d"	"d"	"d"	"d"	"b"	"d"	"d"
0	0.07	0.071	0.072	0.074	0.043	0.073	0.077
5	0.083	0.084	0.083	0.085	0.049	0.086	0.091
10	0.104	0.104	0.104	0.106	0.061	0.106	0.115
15	0.122	0.122	0.122	0.124	0.071	0.125	0.133
20	0.135	0.136	0.136	0.138	0.079	0.139	0.147
25	0.148	0.149	0.149	0.152	0.087	0.152	0.16
30	0.16	0.162	0.162	0.165	0.095	0.165	0.173
35	0.172	0.174	0.175	0.177	0.102	0.178	0.185
40	0.186	0.186	0.187	0.189	0.109	0.194	0.197
45	0.198	0.199	0.2	0.202	0.116	0.207	0.209
50	0.211	0.211	0.212	0.214	0.123	0.219	0.221
55	0.234	0.225	0.227	0.228	0.131	0.232	0.236
60	0.236	0.238	0.239	0.241	0.138	0.245	0.248
65	0.25	0.251	0.253	0.254	0.146	0.259	0.261
70	0.263	0.264	0.266	0.267	0.153	0.272	0.275
75	0.278	0.278	0.28	0.281	0.161	0.289	0.289
80	0.309	0.295	0.285	0.296	0.17	0.306	0.303
85	0.318	0.319	0.33	0.33	0.189	0.313	0.317
90	0.32	0.328	0.34	0.34	0.195	0.351	0.333
95					0.195	0.357	0.366
100						0.363	0.37
105							0.373

Taper Collection: Gillum

Maker	Gillum	Gillum	Gillum
Model		593	86
Length	7'-6"x 2pc	9'-0"	8'-0"
Line Size	5wt		6wt
Station	"d"	"d"	"d"
0	0.071	0.087	0.073
5	0.081	0.102	0.1
10	0.1	0.114	0.118
15	0.116	0.145	0.145
20	0.136	0.157	0.161
25	0.148	0.172	0.175
30	0.161	0.193	0.182
35	0.18	0.207	0.191
40	0.205	0.216	0.203
45	0.215	0.233	0.212
50	0.225	0.243	0.24
55	0.242	0.262	0.256
60	0.254	0.283	0.278
65	0.276	0.293	0.298
70	0.29	0.3	0.309
75	0.292	0.321	0.327
80	0.31	0.333	0.351
85		0.356	0.355
90		0.377	
95		0.387	
100		0.397	
105		0.41	
110		0.43	

Taper Collection: Gould

Maker	Gould	Gould	Gould	Gould	Gould	Gould	Gould	Gould
Model	Shorty	Shorty	Hollow Butt	Hollow	Hollow	Hollow	Hollow	Hollow
Rod No.	RR-133	RR-134	RR-43H	RR-62H	RR-63H	RR-129H	RR-137H	RR-139H
Length	5'-0"x2pc	6'-0"x2pc	7'-6" x 2pc	8'-0" x 2pc	8'-0" x 2pc	8'-0" x 2pc	8'-3" x 2pc	7'-6" x 2pc
Feature			tapered hole	.080 wall	.080 wall	fluted	fluted	fluted
Line Size	4wt	5wt	5wt	5/6wt	5/6wt	7wt	7wt	5wt
Rise	.344xfast	.313xfast	.264 med	.272 med	.256 slow	.284 fast	.284 fast	.288 fast
Station	"d"	"d"	"d"	"d"	"d"	"d"	"d"	"d"
0	0.075	0.088	0.07	0.077	0.079	0.079	0.087	0.08
5	0.091	0.094	0.088	0.091	0.097	0.089	0.092	0.093
10	0.1	0.11	0.107	0.11	0.109	0.115	0.122	0.115
15	0.11	0.124	0.125	0.128	0.124	0.129	0.134	0.133
20	0.123	0.137	0.139	0.142	0.141	0.145	0.156	0.145
25	0.14	0.155	0.153	0.153	0.153	0.159	0.164	0.161
30	0.16	0.175	0.166	0.166	0.169	0.173	0.173	0.177
35	0.183	0.182	0.178	0.178	0.18	0.184	0.186	0.186
40	0.203	0.186	0.189	0.19	0.191	0.199	0.207	0.201
45	0.221	0.21	0.2	0.201	0.205	0.205	0.215	0.207
50	0.243	0.228	0.212	0.215	0.213	0.219	0.222	0.227
55	0.262	0.243	0.226	0.227	0.225	0.237	0.232	0.246
60	0.272	0.267	0.239	0.246	0.237	0.257	0.264	0.259
65		0.283	0.253	0.265	0.262	0.27	0.273	0.272
70		0.292	0.264	0.288	0.283	0.297	0.294	0.284
75		0.298	0.278	0.308	0.308	0.326	0.328	0.306
80			0.309	0.338	0.337	0.356	0.357	0.341
85			0.317	0.353	0.353	0.384	0.384	0.35
90			0.321	0.353	0.354	0.388	0.39	0.343
95				0.353	0.355	0.396	0.389	
100							0.38	

Taper Collection: Gould

Maker	Gould	Gould	Gould	Gould	Gould
Model	Graphite Insert	Graphite Insert	Graphite Insert	Graphite Insert	Graphite Insert
Rod No.	RR-91-8'-3" GI	RR-95-8'-3"GI	RR-96-8'-3" GI	RR-101-9 GI	RR-102-8GI
Length	8'-3" x 2pc	8'-3" x 2pc	8'-3" x 2pc	9'-0" x 3pc	8'-0" x 2pc
Insert	18" located *	18" Located *	55" located *	16" located *	55" located *
Line Size	7wt	7wt	7wt	8wt	6/7wt
Rise	.288 fast	.288 fast	.278 medium	.28 medium	.256 slow
Station	"d"	"d"	"d"	"d"	"d"
0	0.078	0.077	0.078	0.077	0.078
5	0.084	0.084	0.088	0.09	0.088
10	0.102	0.102	0.106	0.105	0.107
15	0.118	0.118	0.121	0.12	0.121
20	0.134	0.134	0.135	0.134	0.135
25	0.146	0.146	0.146	0.15	0.149
30	0.16	0.16	0.159	0.163	0.16
35	0.172	0.172	0.171	0.176	0.173
40	0.184	0.184	0.184	0.19	0.186
45	0.196	0.196	.196 w/.050insert*	0.203	.200 w/.058insert*
50	0.212	0.212	.211 w/.069insert*	0.217	.211 w/.073insert*
55	0.228	0.228	.227 w/.087insert*	0.231	.230 w/.085insert*
60	0.246	0.246	.245 w/.105insert*	0.245	.235 w/.099insert*
65	0.263	0.272	.270 w/.121insert*	0.261	.255 w/.112insert*
70	0.299	0.305	.298 w/.137insert*	0.277	.270 w/.128insert*
75	0.32	0.341	.333 w/.155insert*	0.294	.283 w/.142insert*
80	.340 w/.186insert*	.367 w/.215insert*	.355 w/.171insert*	0.312	.297 w/.158insert*
85	.355 w/.198insert*	.383 w/.227insert*	.367 w/.188insert*	0.332	.310 w/.173insert*
90	.368 w/.216insert*	.394 w/.227insert*	.374 w/.205insert*	.354 w/.213insert*	.325 w/.189insert*
95	.376 w.230insert*	.397 w/.240insert*	.375 w/.218insert*	.375 w/.227insert*	.351 w/.202insert*
100	.380 w/.236insert*	.400 w/.251insert*	.406 w/.260insert*	.385 w/.241insert*	.351 w/.203insert*
105				.415 w/.250insert*	

Taper Collection: Gould

Maker	Gould	Gould	Gould	Gould	Gould
Model	Graphite Insert	Graphite Insert	Graphite Insert	Graphite Insert	Graphite Insert
Rod No.	RR-103-8GI	RR-107-8GI	RR-109-9GI	RR-110-8'-6"GI	RR-115-8'-8"GI
Length	8'-0" x 2pc	8'-0" x 2pc	9'-0" x 3pc	8'-6" x 2pc	8'-8" x 2pc
Insert	45" located *	55" located *	63" located *	55" located *	50" located *
Line Size	7wt	6wt	9wt	6/7wt	6/7wt
Rise	.292 fast	.296 fast	.29 fast	.306xfast	.298 fast
Station	"d"	"d"	"d"	"d"	"d"
0	0.078	0.065	0.077	0.078	0.079
5	0.09	0.083	0.09	0.095	0.099
10	0.111	0.102	0.105	0.107	0.123
15	0.126	0.117	0.12	0.121	0.144
20	0.14	0.133	0.134	0.135	0.159
25	0.154	0.146	0.15	0.15	0.173
30	0.167	0.159	0.163	0.165	0.187
35	0.18	.175 w/.059insert*	0.177	0.18	0.2
40	0.194	.192 w/.079insert*	0.192	0.197	0.214
45	0.208	.206 w/.096insert*	.207 w/.064insert*	.213 w/.055insert*	0.226
50	0.222	.219 w/.108insert*	.220 w/.084insert*	.227 w/.086insert*	.241 w/.083insert*
55	.238 w/.119insert*	.235 w/.122insert*	.234 w/.098insert*	.243 w/.101insert*	.254 w/.094insert*
60	.257 w/.135insert*	.250 w/.135insert*	.250 w/.110insert*	.260 w/.112insert*	.272 w/.112insert*
65	.277 w/.150insert*	.270 w/.149insert*	.262 w/.122insert*	.282 w/.124insert*	.290 w/.128insert*
70	.302 w/.164insert*	.298 w/.161insert*	.276 w/.136insert*	.305 w/.137insert*	.308 w/.146insert*
75	.325 w/.178insert*	.333 w/.173insert*	.289 w.149insert*	.330 w/.149insert*	.328 w/.166insert*
80	.352 w/.192insert*	.355 w/.186insert*	.302 w/.162insert*	.355 w/.162insert*	.354 w/.194insert*
85	.373 w/.207insert*	.367 w/.213insert*	.317 w/.177insert*	.375 w/.174insert*	.379 w/.220insert*
90	.390 w/.221insert*	.387 w/.286insert*	.331 w/.191insert*	.395 w/.186insert*	.398 w/.242insert*
95	.403 w/.298insert*		.345 w/.205insert*	.414 w/.213insert*	.414 w/.260insert*
100			.358 w/.218insert*	.431 w/.291insert*	.422 w/.271insert*
105			.387 w/.267insert*		.422 w/.294insert*
110			.437 w/.317insert*		

Taper Collection: Gould

Maker	Gould	Gould	Gould	Gould	Gould
Model	Graphite Insert	Graphite Insert	Graphite Insert	Graphite Insert	Graphite Insert
Rod No.	RR-117-8'-6"GI	RR-118-8'-3"GI	RR-119-8'-6"GI	RR-122-8'-6"GI	RR-124-8'-6"GI
Length	8'-6" x 2pc	8'-3" x 2pc	8'-6" x 2pc	8'-6" x 2pc	8'-6" x 2pc
Insert	52" located *	20" located *	52" located *	52" located*	22" located *
Line Size	7/8wt	6/7wt	6/7wt	7/8wt	5/6wt
Rise	.286 fast	.288 fast	.286 fast	.286 fast	.276 medium
Station	"d"	"d'	"d"	"d"	"d"
0	0.065	0.066	0.065	0.066	0.064
5	0.083	0.084	0.083	0.084	0.075
10	0.102	0.102	0.102	0.102	0.094
15	0.12	0.118	0.12	0.118	0.113
20	0.136	0.134	0.136	0.134	0.128
25	0.15	0.146	0.15	0.146	0.141
30	0.164	0.16	0.164	0.16	0.154
35	0.178	0.172	0.178	0.172	0.167
40	0.192	0.184	0.192	0.184	0.18
45	0.205	0.196	0.205	0.196	0.193
50	.218 w/.057insert*	0.212	.218 w/.068insert*	.212 w/.069insert*	0.206
55	.231 w/.077insert*	0.228	.231 w/.084insert*	.226 w/.081insert*	0.219
60	.245 w/.092insert*	0.246	.245 w/.098insert*	.245 w/.105insert*	0.232
65	.262 w/.101insert*	0.272	.262 w/.114insert*	.267 w/.127insert*	0.245
70	.282 w/.116insert	0.305	.282 w/.130insert*	.289 w/.149insert*	0.261
75	.310 w/. 131insert*	0.341	.310 w/.149insert*	.311 w/.171insert*	0.279
80	.345 w/.151insert*	.367 w/.216insert*	.345 w/.171insert*	.332 w/.192insert	.295 w/.155insert*
85	.367 w/.177insert*	.383 w/.226insert*	.367 w/.197insert*	.358 w/.218insert*	.313 w/.173insert*
90	.379 w/.198insert*	.394 w/.224insert*	.379 w/.222insert*	.386 w/.246insert*	.330 w/.190insert*
95	.386 w/.219insert*	.397 w/.238insert*	.386 w/.244insert*	.414 w/.274insert*	.337 w/.197insert*
100	.387 w/.237insert*	.400 w/.251insert*	.389 w/.260insert*	.432 w/.292insert*	.338 w/.198insert*
105	.387 w/.262insert*		.393 w/.273insert*	.432 w/.308insert*	.338 w/.198insert*

Taper Collection: Gould

Maker	Gould	Gould	Gould	Gould	Gould
Model	Graphite Insert	Graphite Insert	Graphite Insert	Quad-Chironomid	Quadrate
Rod No.	RR-140-8GI	RR-143-8'-6"GI	RR-152-8'-1"GI	RR-120-8	RR-132-8
Length	8'-0" x 2pc	8'-6" x 3pc	8'-1" x 4pc	8.0" x 2pc	8'-0" x 2pc
Insert	56" Located*	14"hvy wall located*	50" located*		
Line Size	5wt	5wt	5wt	4/5wt	5/6wt
Rise	.288 fast	.28 medium	.29 fast	.266 medium	.25 slow
Station					
"d"	"d"	"d"	"d"	"d"	
0	0.074	0.065	0.068	0.06	0.075
5	0.091	0.079	0.079	0.077	0.086
10	0.108	0.1	0.101	0.095	0.091
15	0.127	0.119	0.12	0.109	0.117
20	0.142	0.14	0.14	0.124	0.128
25	0.156	0.154	0.151	0.136	0.138
30	0.17	0.166	0.162	0.148	0.146
35	0.184	0.166	0.172	0.159	0.156
40	0.197	0.18	0.183	0.171	0.162
45	.210 w/.056insert*	0.195	0.197	0.182	0.177
50	.224 w/.075insert*	0.218	.215 w/.062insert*	0.196	0.195
55	.238 w/.087insert*	0.239	.232 w/.080insert*	0.211	0.196
60	.252 w/.098insert*	0.24	.246 w/.093insert*	0.228	0.216
65	.266 w/.110insert*	0.246	.257 w/.103insert*	0.251	0.245
70	.280 w/.123insert*	0.251	.268 w/.115insert*	0.277	0.263
75	.294 w/.142insert*	0.273	.283 w/.125insert*	0.31	0.298
80	.316 w/.160insert*	0.291	.300 w/.140insert*	0.331	0.316
85	.344 w/.176insert*	0.309	.317 w/.157insert*	0.342	0.329
90	.347 w/.194insert*	.355 w/..182insert*	.332 w/.193insert*	0.248	0.337
95	.347 w/.210insert*	.412 w/.202insert*	.348 w/.209insert*	0.349	0.347
100	.347 w/.212insert*	.413 w/.220insert*	.348 w/.224insert*	0.349	
105		.414 w/.225insert*			

Fig. 80: Gould's Quadrate RR-132-8.

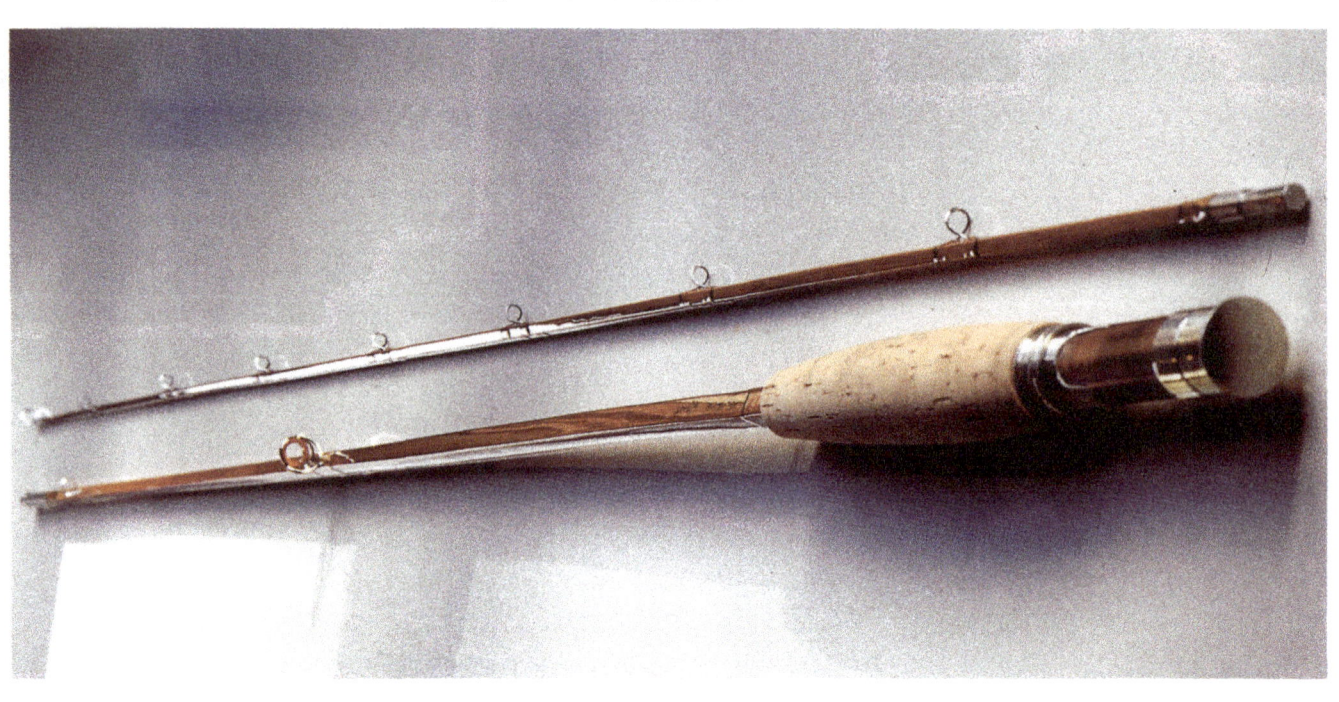

Taper Collection: Gould

Maker	Gould	Gould	Gould	Gould	Gould
Model	7 Series	7 Series	7 Series	My pet	Strong Special
Rod No.	RR-25,26,27	RR-58	RR-94	RR-108	RR-135,136
Length	7'-0" x 2pc	7'-0" x 2pc	7'-0" x 2pc	7'-0" x 2pc	7'-0" x 2pc
Feature	Med Action	w/butt swell	Med action	Med action	fast action
Line Size	4wt	5wt	5wt	4wt	4wt
Rise	.264 medium	.264 medium	.28 medium	.274 medium	.316xfast
Station	"d"	"d"	"d"	"d"	"d"
0	0.07	0.07	0.077	0.067	0.075
5	0.088	0.088	0.096	0.077	0.1
10	0.107	0.107	0.109	0.095	0.117
15	0.125	0.125	0.13	0.112	0.13
20	0.139	0.139	0.146	0.127	0.15
25	0.153	0.153	0.164	0.14	0.165
30	0.166	0.166	0.178	0.153	0.178
35	0.178	0.178	0.194	0.166	0.195
40	0.189	0.189	0.203	0.179	0.212
45	0.2	0.2	0.213	0.192	0.225
50	0.212	0.212	0.224	0.205	0.232
55	0.226	0.226	0.236	0.218	0.255
60	0.239	0.239	0.249	0.232	0.275
65	0.253	0.253	0.268	0.25	0.292
70	0.264	0.272	0.296	0.271	0.317
75	0.278	0.295	0.318	0.294	0.335
80	0.291	0.302	0.327	0.294	grip
85	0.304	0.31	0.331	0.294	grip

Fig. 81: Chamberlain's fly-tying case lid.

Taper Collection: Gould

Maker	Gould	Gould	Gould	Gould	Gould	Gould	Gould
Model	G209	G209A	Dutchess	J.Enerson	G206	Light Para	Rogowski
Rod No.	RR-30to40	RR-31	RR-50,51	RR-67,70,79	RR-74	RR-82	RR-93
Length	7'-6" x 2pc	7'-6" x 2pc	7'-6" x 2pc	7'-6" x 2pc	7'-6" x 2pc	7'-6" x2pc	7'-6" x 2pc
Feature	Med action	Med action	Med action	Med action	Butt swell	Med action	Fast action
Line Size	5wt	5wt	5/6wt	5/6wt	5/6wt	6wt	4wt
Rise	.264 medium	.266 medium	.276 medium	.264 medium	.266 medium	.276 medium	.308xfast
Station	"d"	"d"	"d"	"d"	"d"	"d"	"d"
0	0.07	0.073	0.07	0.07	0.067	0.065	0.065
5	0.088	0.083	0.088	0.088	0.078	0.083	0.081
10	0.107	0.107	0.107	0.107	0.1	0.103	0.091
15	0.125	0.124	0.125	0.125	0.117	0.12	0.118
20	0.139	0.14	0.139	0.139	0.131	0.135	0.133
25	0.153	0.155	0.153	0.153	0.144	0.149	0.148
30	0.166	0.165	0.166	0.166	0.156	0.161	0.162
35	0.178	0.18	0.178	0.178	0.168	0.174	0.177
40	0.189	0.191	0.189	0.189	0.181	0.186	0.191
45	0.2	0.203	0.205	0.2	0.194	0.198	0.204
50	0.212	0.211	0.217	0.212	0.206	0.212	0.218
55	0.226	0.228	0.232	0.226	0.22	0.227	0.232
60	0.239	0.24	0.245	0.239	0.233	0.241	0.245
65	0.253	0.254	0.264	0.253	0.25	0.255	0.259
70	0.264	0.264	0.281	0.273	0.268	0.272	0.277
75	0.278	0.278	0.296	0.298	0.295	0.29	0.3
80	0.309	0.308	0.315	0.327	0.307	0.318	0.317
85	0.317	0.318	0.332	0.343	0.313	0.335	0.327
90	0.32	0.322	0.35	0.35	0.316	0.34	0.334

Taper Collection: Gould

Maker	Gould	Gould	Gould	Gould	Gould	Gould	Gould
Model	Long hand	Mooner	Chowder1	Glffdmppc	R.Young	Standby	M.Skeith
Rod. No.	RR-2-8	RR-3,4	RR-6,7	RR-8 to 14	RR-15	RR-18,28	RR-20
Length	8'-0" x 2pc	8'-0" x 2pc	8'-0" x 2pc	8'-0" x 2pc	8'-0" x 2pc	8'-0" x 2pc	8'-0" x 2pc
Feature		Slow action	Slow action	Slow action	Slow action	Slow Action	
Line Size	8wt	7wt	6wt	6wt	6wt	6/7wt	6/7wt
Rise	.294 fast	.202 xslow	.216 xslow	.216 xslow	.216 xslow	.244 slow	.262 med
Station	"d"	"d"	"d"	"d"	"d"	"d"	"d"
0	0.07	0.08	0.08	0.08	0.08	0.08	0.081
5	0.091	0.116	0.113	0.113	0.113	0.113	0.112
10	0.117	0.131	0.13	0.13	0.13	0.13	0.132
15	0.136	0.148	0.148	0.148	0.148	0.148	0.149
20	0.152	0.157	0.16	0.16	0.16	0.16	0.171
25	0.167	0.164	0.172	0.172	0.172	0.172	0.179
30	0.182	0.172	0.18	0.18	0.182	0.183	0.193
35	0.195	0.173	0.185	0.185	0.188	0.193	0.204
40	0.208	0.188	0.19	0.19	0.197	0.203	0.21
45	0.221	0.19	0.2	0.2	0.205	0.213	0.218
50	0.234	0.22	0.21	0.21	0.213	0.225	0.233
55	0.25	0.228	0.225	0.225	0.225	0.238	0.245
60	0.264	0.232	0.238	0.238	0.238	0.252	0.263
65	0.278	0.251	0.252	0.252	0.255	0.268	0.276
70	0.292	0.262	0.268	0.268	0.274	0.283	0.292
75	0.307	0.282	0.283	0.29	0.293	0.3	0.307
80	0.322	0.298	0.302	0.315	0.32	0.32	0.327
85	0.35	0.335	0.32	0.333	0.345	0.345	0.353
90	0.36	0.345	0.335	0.345	0.352	0.352	0.367
95	0.37	0.345	0.345	0.355	0.355	0.355	0.367
100			0.355	0.355	0.355	0.355	

Taper Collection: Gould

Maker	Gould	Gould	Gould	Gould	Gould	Gould	Gould
Model		H203	212/203	MAG	SEG		McConnell
Rod No.	RR-29	RR-52	RR-53,54,55	RR-59,60,61,66	RR-64,65	RR-67,68	RR-71,72,73
Length	8'-0" x 2pc	8'-0" x 2pc	8'-0" x 2pc	8'-0" x 2pc	8'-0" x 2pc	8'-0" x 2pc	8'-0" x 2pc
Feature	Slow Action	Med Action	Med Action	Butt swell	Slow action	Butt swell	Butt swell
Line Size	6/7wt	6/7wt	6/7wt	6/7wt	6/7wt	6/7wt	6/7wt
Rise	.252 slow	.28 medium	.272 medium	.272 medium	.216 xslow	0.260 slow	0.260 slow
Station	"d"	"d"	"d"	"d"	"d"	"d"	"d"
0	0.085	0.075	0.075	0.075	0.08	0.07	0.07
5	0.108	0.083	0.09	0.09	0.113	0.088	0.088
10	0.125	0.102	0.107	0.107	0.13	0.107	0.109
15	0.14	0.118	0.122	0.122	0.148	0.125	0.127
20	0.157	0.133	0.136	0.136	0.16	0.139	0.14
25	0.172	0.148	0.149	0.149	0.172	0.153	0.153
30	0.185	0.163	0.162	0.162	0.18	0.166	0.167
35	0.194	0.176	0.175	0.175	0.185	0.176	0.178
40	0.205	0.188	0.187	0.187	0.193	0.189	0.189
45	0.214	0.199	0.198	0.198	0.2	0.2	0.2
50	0.225	0.216	0.211	0.211	0.211	0.212	0.212
55	0.237	0.228	0.227	0.227	0.233	0.226	0.226
60	0.252	0.242	0.243	0.243	0.238	0.239	0.239
65	0.265	0.265	0.263	0.263	0.257	0.253	0.254
70	0.277	0.288	0.283	0.283	0.275	0.273	0.275
75	0.288	0.302	0.303	0.303	0.294	0.298	0.305
80	0.305	0.327	0.326	0.337	0.315	0.327	0.333
85	0.333	0.347	0.344	0.348	0.333	0.343	0.344
90	0.35	0.372	0.35	0.35	0.315	0.35	0.353
95	0.355	0.39	0.35	0.35	0.356	0.35	0.353

Fig. 82: Net by Bruce Johnson.

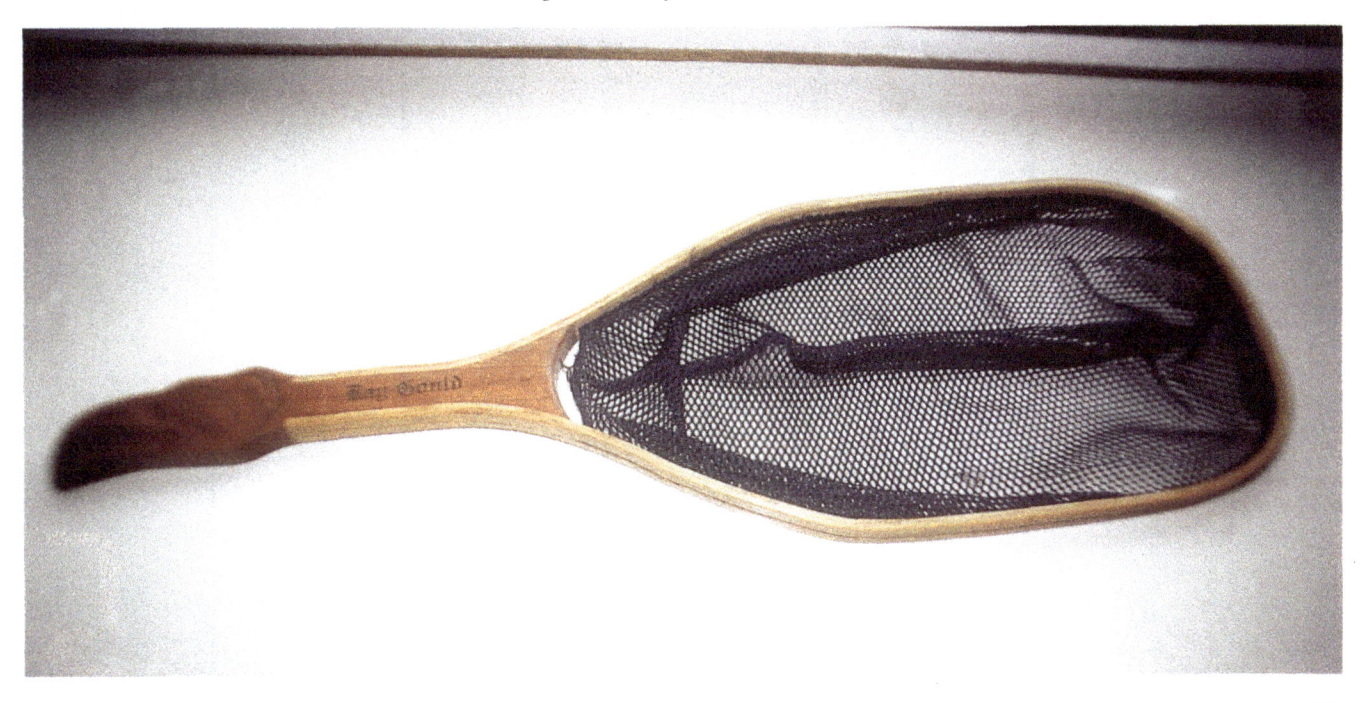

Taper Collection: Gould

Maker	Gould	Gould	Gould	Gould	Gould	Gould	Gould
Model	NWWFF	Favorite	Myerson	Lwulff	Benzel	CRB	Huff
Rod No.	RR-83	RR84-88,104,138	RR-97	RR-98	RR-105	RR-106	RR-116
Length	8'-0" x 2pc	8'-0" x 2pc	8'-0" x 2pc	8'-0" x 2pc	8'-0" x 2pc	8/-0" x 2pc	8'-0" x 2pc
Feature		Butt swell	Med Action	Butt swell	Butt swell		
Line size	6/7wt	6/7wt	4wt	5/6wt	6/7wt	6/7wt	4/5wt
Rise	0.286 fast	.286 fast	.274 medium	.290 fast	.280 medium	.304xfast	.268 medium
Station	"d"	"d"	"d"	"d"	"d"	"d"	"d"
0	0.065	0.065	0.075	0.077	0.078	0.083	0.066
5	0.083	0.083	0.091	0.095	0.086	0.089	0.078
10	0.102	0.102	0.107	0.113	0.105	0.109	0.098
15	0.119	0.117	0.125	0.128	0.117	0.122	0.115
20	0.133	0.133	0.14	0.144	0.133	0.133	0.129
25	0.146	0.146	0.153	0.159	0.153	0.151	0.143
30	0.159	0.159	0.166	0.173	0.162	0.161	0.155
35	0.171	0.171	0.179	0.187	0.176	0.169	0.168
40	0.184	0.184	0.191	0.2	0.185	0.181	0.181
45	0.196	0.196	0.204	0.214	0.199	0.197	0.193
50	0.209	0.211	0.217	0.229	0.215	0.221	0.206
55	0.227	0.227	0.231	0.243	0.227	0.235	0.219
60	0.245	0.245	0.244	0.258	0.245	0.261	0.232
65	0.265	0.27	0.257	0.272	0.27	0.275	0.245
70	0.287	0.298	0.27	0.29	0.298	0.318	0.258
75	0.312	0.333	0.283	0.31	0.333	0.352	0.271
80	0.33	0.355	0.296	0.332	0.355	0.373	0.286
85	0.341	0.367	0.309	0.348	0.367	0.385	0.3
90	0.35	0.374	0.322	0.357	0.374	0.381	0.314
95	0.353	0.375	0.336	0.362	0.375	0.385	0.328

Taper Collection: Gould

Maker	Gould	Gould	Gould	Gould	Gould	Gould
Model	BigMac	Wagner	Edwards	G212E	G212E	Jwulff
Rod No.	RR-128	RR-130	RR-131	RR-148	RR-149	RR-151
Length	8'-0" x 2pc	8'-0" x 2pc	8'-0" x 3pc	8'-0" x 2pc	8'-0" x 2pc	8'-0" x 3pc
Feature	med action	med action	slow action	fast action	fast action	fast action
Line Size	4wt	6/7wy	3/4wt	4/5wt	6wt	5wt
Rise	.256slow	.278 Med	.248 slow	.284fast	.290 fast	.290fast
Station	"d"	"d"	"d"	"d"	"d"	"d"
0	0.075	0.08	0.07	0.07	0.07	0.068
5	0.09	0.105	0.084	0.09	0.09	0.079
10	0.1	0.126	0.107	0.103	0.105	0.101
15	0.11	0.146	0.119	0.115	0.115	0.12
20	0.126	0.161	0.132	0.132	0.13	0.14
25	0.138	0.175	0.147	0.153	0.15	0.151
30	0.16	0.19	0.152	0.17	0.167	0.162
35	0.167	0.203	0.153	0.181	0.18	0.172
40	0.18	0.215	0.169	0.189	0.192	0.182
45	0.19	0.227	0.187	0.197	0.201	0.197
50	0.199	0.24	0.205	0.21	0.212	0.215
55	0.219	0.25	0.216	0.228	0.23	0.232
60	0.228	0.265	0.231	0.245	0.25	0.246
65	0.249	0.283	0.245	0.258	0.27	0.257
70	0.264	0.298	0.271	0.268	0.29	0.268
75	0.283	0.314	0.285	0.281	0.308	0.283
80	0.294	0.34	0.302	0.301	0.322	0.3
85	0.308	0.354	0.377	0.32	0.34	0.317
90	0.32	0.358	0.42	0.33	0.348	0.332
95	0.333	0.375	0.42	0.33	0.35	0.348

Taper Collection: Gould

Maker	Gould	Gould	Gould	Gould	Gould	Gould
Model		G215	H310		Keever	Chironomid2
Rod No.	RR-19	RR-41	RR75,76	RR81	RR99	RR-100
Length	8'-6" x 3pc	8'-6" x 3pc	8'-6" x 2pc	8'-6" x 2pc	8'-6" x 2pc	8'-6" x 2pc
Feature	xslow action	med action	fast action	med action	med action	med action
Line size	6/7wt	6wt	8/9wt	6wt	5/6wt	6wt
Rise	.230xslow	.266medium	.284fast	.272 medium	.272 medium	.274 medium
Station	"d"	"d"	"d"	"d"	"d"	"d"
0	0.08	0.076	0.07	0.07	0.08	0.077
5	0.113	0.096	0.087	0.089	0.095	0.097
10	0.13	0.112	0.105	0.103	0.11	0.115
15	0.148	0.125	0.12	0.12	0.125	0.132
20	0.16	0.139	0.135	0.135	0.14	0.147
25	0.175	0.152	0.15	0.149	0.153	0.166
30	0.185	0.165	0.165	0.162	0.167	0.175
35	0.195	0.178	0.177	0.174	0.18	0.188
40	0.205	0.194	0.192	0.186	0.192	0.202
45	0.215	0.207	0.205	0.199	0.205	0.214
50	0.225	0.219	0.217	0.211	0.219	0.227
55	0.235	0.232	0.232	0.225	0.232	0.24
60	0.245	0.245	0.247	0.239	0.246	0.252
65	0.265	0.259	0.265	0.254	0.259	0.265
70	0.287	0.272	0.283	0.267	0.272	0.28
75	0.305	0.285	0.303	0.282	0.286	0.297
80	0.32	0.298	0.323	0.297	0.299	0.317
85	0.35	0.313	0.343	0.313	0.313	0.325
90	0.385	0.351	0.364	0.333	0.326	0.35
95	0.385	0.355	0.387	0.35	0.339	0.36
100	0.385	0.36	0.41	0.363	0.352	0.363
105	0.385	0.363	0.42	0.366	0.354	0.365

Taper Collection: Gould & Granger

Maker	Gould	Gould	Gould	Granger	Granger	Granger	Granger
Model	H308		Steelhead	9050	9053	Victory	Aristocrat
Rod No.	RR-111	RR-112	RR-113,114				
Length	8'-6" x 2pc	8'-6" x 2pc	9'-0" x 3pc	9'-0"	9'-0"	7'-0"	7'-0"
Feature	butt swell	med action	med action				
Line Size	6/7wt	5/6wt	6wt	DT6wt		5wt	
Rise	.286 fast	.280 med	.276 med				
Station "d"	"d"	"d"	"d"	"d"	"d"	"d"	"d"
0	0.065	0.067	0.07	0.085	0.099	0.07	0.062
5	0.083	0.078	0.087	0.091	0.107	0.072	0.072
10	0.102	0.098	0.109	0.105	0.131	0.09	0.092
15	0.12	0.117	0.129	0.12	0.148	0.105	0.108
20	0.136	0.132	0.144	0.14	0.16	0.12	0.12
25	0.15	0.146	0.158	0.155	0.177	0.13	0.135
30	0.164	0.159	0.171	0.166	0.194	0.144	0.145
35	0.178	0.172	0.185	0.17	0.202	0.156	0.158
40	0.192	0.185	0.197	0.202	0.229	0.168	0.17
45	0.205	0.198	0.21	0.221	0.249	0.18	0.196
50	0.218	0.211	0.223	0.237	0.265	0.2	0.21
55	0.231	0.225	0.235	0.245	0.269	0.203	0.229
60	0.245	0.238	0.247	0.253	0.28	0.225	0.241
65	0.257	0.252	0.26	0.257	0.288	0.239	0.253
70	0.282	0.262	0.272	0.258	0.296	0.245	0.262
75	0.31	0.279	0.284	0.285	0.324	0.26	0.271
80	0.345	0.293	0.3	0.298	0.34	0.27	0.284
85	0.367	0.308	0.217	0.311	0.351	0.335	0.32
90	0.379	0.323	0.335	0.326	0.359		0.336
95	0.386	0.337	0.35	0.337	0.371		
100	0.387	0.351	0.36	0.401			
105	0.387	0.357	0.37				
110			0.374				

Fig. 83: Granger Victory ink work.

Taper Collection: Granger, Halstead

Maker	Granger	Granger	Granger	Granger	Halstead	Halstead	Halstead
Model	Special	Favorite	Aristocrat	Aristocrat	3pc	3pc	
Length	7'-6"	8'-0"	8'-6"	9'-0"	8'-6"	8'-6" another	7'-6"
Line Size							5wt
Station	"d"	"d"	"d"	"d"	"d"	"d"	"d"
0	0.068	0.07	0.062	0.062	0.071	0.072	0.065
5	0.083	0.084	0.073	0.075	0.087	0.087	0.077
10	0.098	0.101	0.092	0.091	0.098	0.098	0.097
15	0.115	0.118	0.109	0.112	0.103	0.106	0.115
20	0.132	0.131	0.122	0.128	0.126	0.126	0.132
25	0.145	0.145	0.137	0.144	0.145	0.146	0.146
30	0.16	0.154	0.15	0.159	0.142	0.146	0.15
35	0.176	0.169	0.168	0.171	0.166	0.165	0.167
40	0.189	0.186	0.187	0.194	0.19	0.184	0.187
45	0.201	0.199	0.206	0.215	0.201	0.2	0.203
50	0.218	0.21	0.22	0.23	0.219	0.216	0.215
55	0.234	0.217	0.232	0.241	0.231	0.227	0.227
60	0.246	0.223	0.24	0.252	0.237	0.243	0.235
65	0.258	0.241	0.245	0.259	0.255	0.255	0.256
70	0.271	0.26	0.264	0.263	0.26	0.27	0.28
75	0.283	0.273	0.283	0.279	0.264	0.268	0.305
80	0.331	0.288	0.29	0.294	0.292	0.287	0.328
85	0.331	0.331	0.306	0.311	0.309	0.305	0.345
90	0.331	0.358	0.318	0.325	0.317	0.315	
95		0.358	0.371	0.332	0.376		
100		0.358	0.38	handle			
105			0.38	handle			

Taper Collection: Hardy

Maker	Hardy	Hardy	Hardy	Hardy	Hardy	Hardy	Hardy	Hardy
Model	CCdeFrance	Palakona	Wye	Phantom	Phantom	Phantom	A&F Banty	CCdeFrance
Length	8'-0" x 2pc	8'-9"	11'-0"	8'-0"	8'-0" x 2pc	8'-6"	4'-0"	9'-0"
Line Size	5wt	7wt	F2AE	5wt	5wt	6wt		5/6wt
Station					Hollokona	Hollokona		
	"d"	"d"	"d"	"d"	"d"	"d"	"d"	"d"
0	0.062	0.09	0.116	0.078	0.078	0.08	0.07	0.085
5	0.093	0.099	0.132	0.092	0.093	0.102	0.088	0.1
10	0.114	0.113	0.153	0.113	0.11	0.122	0.107	0.123
15	0.135	0.134	0.174	0.129	0.125	0.139	0.119	0.151
20	0.149	0.15	0.185	0.142	0.14	0.152	0.133	0.165
25	0.161	0.167	0.196	0.148	0.154	0.169	0.146	0.177
30	0.173	0.185	0.208	0.168	0.164	0.183	0.175	0.188
35	0.184	0.197	0.221	0.187	0.174	0.192	0.182	0.198
40	0.198	0.212	234	0.189	0.184	0.202	0.198	0.213
45	0.207	0.225	0.264	0.204	0.193	0.216	0.205	0.219
50	0.218	0.234	0.267	0.227	0.207	0.23		0.231
55	0.228	0.258	0.285	0.245	0.23	0.25		0.245
60	0.241	0.274	0.299	0.262	0.243	0.26		0.256
65	0.255	0.284	0.313	0.273	0.255	0.27		0.269
70	0.261	0.3	0.323	0.289	0.268	0.285		0.281
75	0.276	0.31	0.335	0.305	0.283	0.3		0.244
80	0.291	0.322	0.347	0.32	0.3	0.313		0.304
85	0.297	0.333	0.368	0.333	0.316	0.33		0.312
90	0.321	0.345	0.383	0.348	handle	0.34		0.324
95	0.333	0.397	0.396	0.364	handle	handle		0.332
100		handle	0.405			handle		handle
105		handle	0.417					handle
110			0.43					
115			handle					
120			handle					
125			handle					
130			handle					

Taper Collection: Hardy, Heddon

Maker	Hardy	Hardy	Heddon	Heddon	Heddon	Heddon	Heddon
Model	Special	Fairchild	#1650	#850	#851L	#10	#20 Bill Stanley
Length	9'-6" x 3pc	8'-6" x 3pc	8-6" x 2pc	6'-0" x 1pc	5'-6" x 1pc	8'-6"x2 1/2F	7'-6"
Line Size			Casting Rod	Bait Caster	Bait Caster	HCH	5wt
Station			Steelhead				
"d"	"d"	"d"	"d"	"d"	"d"	"d"	"d"
0	0.082	0.076	0.112	0.11	0.11	0.075	0.077
5	0.095	0.092	0.133	0.12	0.124	0.092	0.087
10	0.114	0.107	0.156	0.13	0.142	0.106	0.104
15	0.133	0.123	0.18	0.144	0.162	0.116	0.116
20	0.151	0.134	0.201	0.162	0.178	0.133	0.127
25	0.163	0.145	0.225	0.182	0.196	0.143	0.142
30	0.178	0.156	0.243	0.198	0.214	0.158	0.157
35	0.194	0.174	0.271	0.208	0.232	0.179	0.173
40	0.217	0.186	0.295	0.228	0.248	0.2	0.181
45	0.233	0.195	0.318	0.24	0.264	0.218	0.193
50	0.249	0.202	0.344	0.274	0.286	0.232	0.215
55	0.26	0.212	0.361	swell	0.296	0.247	0.233
60	0.276	0.224	0.392			0.261	0.247
65	0.288	0.239	0.427			0.282	0.257
70	0.297	0.243	0.461			0.285	0.271
75	0.303	0.259	0.491			0.302	0.284
80	0.307	0.277	handle			0.318	0.387
85	0.312	0.288	handle			0.327	handle
90	0.333	0.309	handle			0.366	handle
95	0.347	handle	handle			handle	
100	0.367	handle	handle			handle	
105	0.381						
110	handle						
115	handle						

Taper Collection: Heddon

Maker	Heddon	Heddon	Heddon	Heddon	Heddon	Heddon
Model	#17 ExtraLite	Folsum	#14 x 3pc	#17Black Beauty	Black Beauty	#125 x 3pc
Length	8'-0"x 1F	7'-0" x 2pc	8'-0" x 1 3/4F	9'-0" x 3pc	8'-6" x 3pc	8'-0"x 1 3/4F
Line Size	3wt x 3pc	4wt		5/6wt	6wt	
Station						
	"d"	"d"	"d"	"d"	"d"	"d"
0	0.062	0.067	0.08	0.067	0.075	0.073
5	0.069	0.079	0.097	0.079	0.085	0.088
10	0.089	0.088	0.114	0.101	0.101	0.104
15	0.102	0.108	0.126	0.114	0.114	0.114
20	0.117	0.123	0.135	0.126	0.13	0.129
25	0.126	0.141	0.149	0.141	0.141	0.143
30	0.148	0.155	0.16	0.155	0.155	0.158
35	0.163	0.169	0.172	0.17	0.172	0.167
40	0.185	0.18	0.187	0.173	0.185	0.186
45	0.197	0.186	0.205	0.188	0.2	0.202
50	0.211	0.202	0.22	0.205	0.214	0.217
55	0.221	0.22	0.234	0.216	0.231	0.233
60	0.227	0.234	0.25	0.234	0.245	0.25
65	0.249	0.248	0.258	0.249	0.255	0.263
70	0.263	0.265	0.276	0.259	0.287	0.27
75	0.269	0.335	0.288	0.263	0.298	0.286
80	0.287		0.299	0.278	0.309	swell 0.300
85	0.343		0.4	0.292	0.317	0.408
90	handle			0.306	0.37	
95	handle			0.322		
100				0.408		
105				0.437		
110				0.437		

Fig. 84: Heddon #10.

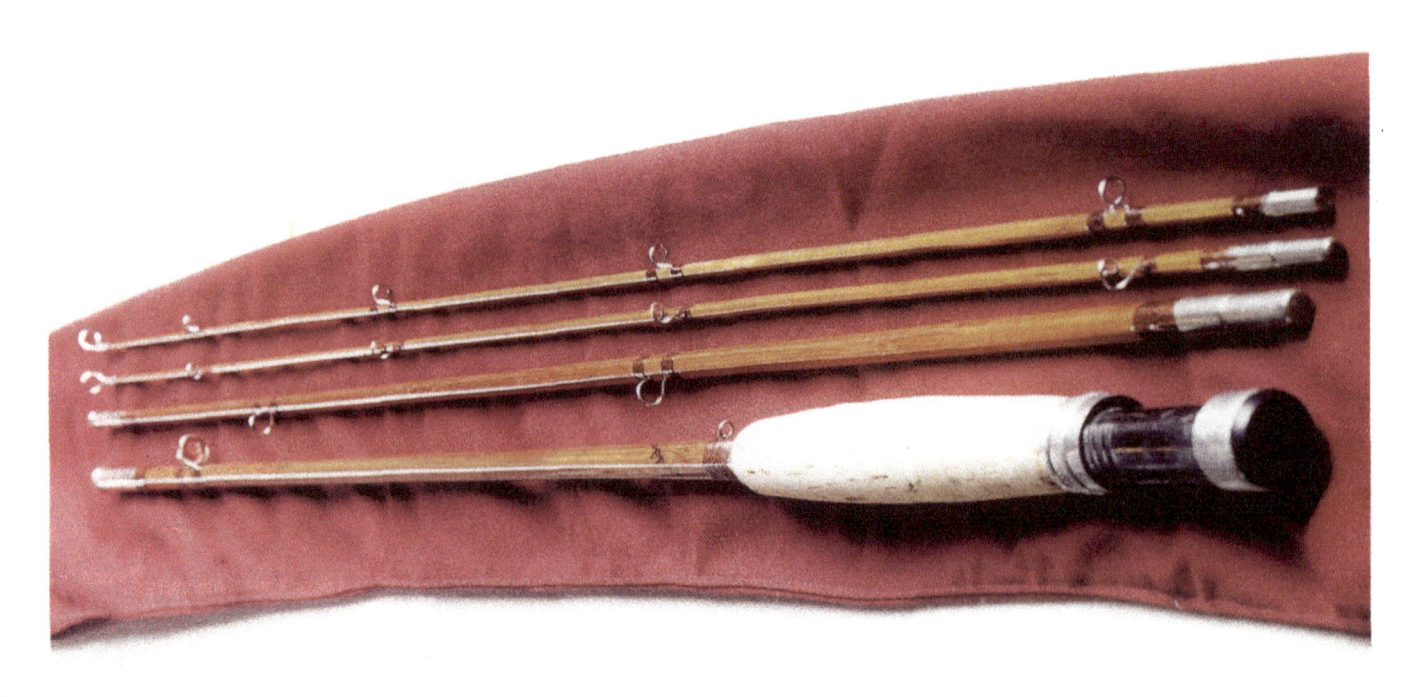

Taper Collection: Herters, Higham, Holbrook

Maker	Herters	Higham	Holbrook	Holbrook	Holbrook	Holbrook	Holbrook
Model			91	#100	197	308	310
Length	5'-6"	6'-0"	7'-0" x 2pc	8'-0" x 2pc	7'-6" x 2pc	8'-6" x 2pc	8'-6" x 2pc
Line Size	Casting Rod	6/7wt	7wt			8wt	9wt
Station		"d"	"d"	"d"	"d"	'd'	
0	0.13	0.07	0.058	0.065	0.062	0.068	0.07
5	0.134	0.09	0.075	0.077	0.079	0.086	0.097
10	0.158	0.103	0.092	0.089	0.096	0.102	0.105
15	0.185	0.122	0.108	0.103	0.112	0.118	0.12
20	0.212	0.139	0.122	0.122	0.126	0.133	0.139
25	0.237	0.153	0.138	0.139	0.142	0.15	0.152
30	0.267	0.172	0.152	0.158	0.156	0.164	0.166
35	0.293	0.184	0.165	0.167	0.17	0.177	0.18
40	0.31	0.19	0.177	0.187	0.183	0.193	0.194
45	0.328	0.206	0.192	0.216	0.196	0.204	0.206
50	0.36	0.228	0.21	0.207	0.21	0.213	0.218
55	0.374	0.248	0.23	0.213	0.227	0.225	0.231
60	0.374	0.259	0.25	0.228	0.246	0.24	0.248
65	0.374	0.27	0.271	0.254	0.266	0.256	0.266
70		0.276	0.294	0.273	0.288	0.272	0.286
75		72 0.288	0.316	0.286	0.31	0.296	0.304
80			0.34	0.312	0.334	0.319	0.324
85			84 0.360	0.331	0.358	0.343	0.345
90				handle	0.38	0.366	0.366
95				handle		0.39	0.389
100						0.412	0.412
105						0.417	102 0.419

Taper Collection: Holbrook, Horgard, Horrocks, Ibbotson

Maker	Holbrook	Horgard	Horgard	Horgard	H.I.	H.I.	H.I.
Model	414	HC	Tana	Alta	Roosevelt	Tonka Queen	Spinner
Length	9'-0" x2pc	12'-0"	13'-6"	14'-0" x 3pc	9'-0" x 3pc	7'-9" x 2pc	9'-0" x 3pc
Line Size	9wt	8/9wt	10wt	10wt			
Station							
	"d"	"d"	"d"	"d"	"d"	"d"	"d"
0	0.07	0.1	0.1	0.125	0.083	0.074	0.095
5	0.086	0.12	0.12	0.145	0.094	0.093	0.104
10	0.104	0.135	0.15	0.166	0.113	0.106	0.117
15	0.118	0.15	0.17	0.186	0.131	0.126	0.133
20	0.135	0.167	0.202	0.21	0.151	0.138	0.144
25	0.151	0.183	0.215	0.225	0.163	0.154	0.156
30	0.164	0.2	0.228	0.244	0.178	0.166	0.187
35	0.18	0.22	0.237	0.264	0.201	0.178	0.27
40	0.194	0.235	0.253	0.28	0.222	0.19	0.221
45	0.206	0.25	0.27	0.3	0.232	0.202	0.231
50	0.219	0.278	0.286	0.315	0.232	0.234	0.239
55	0.232	0.29	0.3	0.32	0.249	0.246	0.25
60	0.244	0.305	0.332	0.355	0.26	0.258	0.26
65	0.26	0.325	0.352	0.38	0.276	0.27	0.276
70	0.277	0.333	0.375	0.398	0.281	0.282	0.282
75	0.296	0.345	0.391	0.41	0.303	0.294	0.321
80	0.312	0.36	0.409	0.43	0.332	0.306	0.343
85	0.334	0.373	0.425	0.445	0.343		0.362
90	0.354	0.387	0.442	0.46	0.356		0.382
95	0.376	0.403	0.458	0.477	0.37		0.397
100	0.397	0.438	0.472	0.5	handle		handle
105	0.42	0.461	0.496	0.524	handle		handle
110	108 0.432	0.48	0.51	0.543			
115		0.499	0.547	0.555			
120		0.515	0.564	0.567			
125		0.53	0.583	0.58			
130		0.552	0.6	0.597			
135		0.57	0.617	0.615			
140		0.59		0.633			
145		0.6					

Taper Collection: Kreider, Leonard

Maker	Kreider	Leonard	Leonard	Leonard	Leonard	Leonard	Leonard
Model	Pentagonal	ACM	36H/37H	38ACM	37H	38H	38H
Length	7'-6"	6'-6" x 2pc	6'-0" x2pc	7'-0" x 2pc	6'-6" x 2pc	7'-0"	7'-0"
Line Size	by Faggetter		3wt	4wt	4wt	4wt	5/6wt
Station	Center to flat						
	"b"	"d"	"d"	"d"	"d"	"d"	"d"
0	0.031	0.04	0.061	0.066	0.06	0.064	0.074
5	0.04	0.055	0.07	0.077	0.076	0.08	0.087
10	0.047	0.067	0.083	0.091	0.102	0.092	0.102
15	0.055	0.085	0.094	0.104	0.112	0.105	0.114
20	0.065	0.104	0.108	0.116	0.13	0.118	0.127
25	0.075	0.111	0.122	0.128	0.141	0.13	0.141
30	0.082	0.128	0.132	0.14	0.155	0.14	0.154
35	0.087	0.132	0.141	0.151	0.163	0.148	0.16
40	0.093	0.146	0.148	0.163	0.172	0.156	0.168
45	0.1	0.16	0.163	0.178	0.181	0.181	0.187
50	0.106	0.176	0.173	0.193	0.192	0.198	0.205
55	0.114	0.195	0.186	0.202	0.212	0.212	0.217
60	0.123	0.215	0.197	0.217	0.228	0.223	0.232
65	0.127	0.225	0.206	0.231	0.241	0.235	0.243
70	0.132	0.31		0.245	0.253	0.25	swell 0.257
75	0.137			0.257	0.281	0.272	swell 0.322
80	0.14			0.27	handle	0.29	swell 0.347
85	0.142			0.282		0.3	swell 0.350
90	0.143						

Fig. 85: Leonard Baby Catskill 7-foot Model 38ACM.

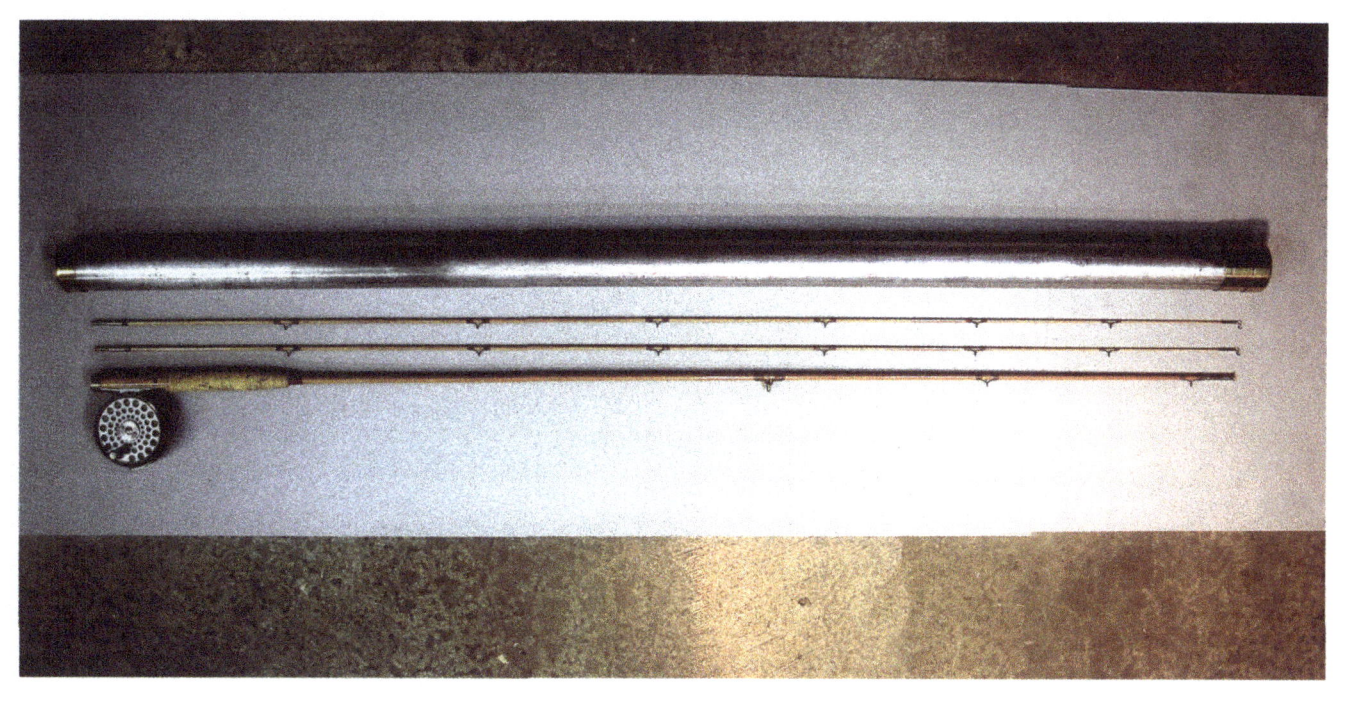

Taper Collection: Leonard

Maker	Leonard	Leonard	Leonard	Leonard	Leonard	Leonard
Model	39	50DF	51HW	Catskill	Baby catskill	
Length	8'-0"	8'-0"	9'-0" x 3pc	8'-2" x 3pc	7'-0" x 2pc	8'-0" x 2pc
Line Size	3wt	6wt		2wt	2/3wt	6wt
Station						
"d"	"d"	"d"	"d"	"d"	"d"	"d"
0	0.048	0.067	0.073	0.043	0.05	0.07
5	0.063	0.097	0.093	0.053	0.055	0.089
10	0.071	0.112	0.115	0.07	0.065	0.113
15	0.087	0.127	0.134	0.08	0.07	0.121
20	0.103	0.132	0.15	0.1	0.09	0.136
25	0.109	0.147	0.165	0.11	0.105	0.145
30	0.118	0.159	0.179	0.125	0.115	0.156
35	0.125	0.17	0.191	0.13	0.125	0.174
40	0.14	0.177	0.2	0.14	0.13	0.182
45	0.154	0.19	0.217	0.15	0.145	0.201
50	0.165	0.202	0.233	0.165	0.157	0.218
55	0.173	0.215	0.245	0.18	0.163	0.23
60	0.179	0.226	0.254	0.21	0.173	0.242
65	0.188	0.242	0.263	0.225	0.187	0.253
70	0.196	0.258	0.275	0.23	swell 0.201	0.267
75	0.213	0.267	0.286	0.245	swell 0.235	0.281
80	0.224	0.28	0.303	84 0.265	swell 0.270	0.304
85	0.245	0.29	0.323	handle	84 0.280	0.311
90	0.288	0.305	0.335	handle		0.32
95	0.288	0.32	0.43	handle		0.32
100	0.288	0.321	0.454			
105			0.454			
110			0.454			

Fig. 87: Leonard Special Tournament 9 1/2-foot, 3-piece x 2 tip.

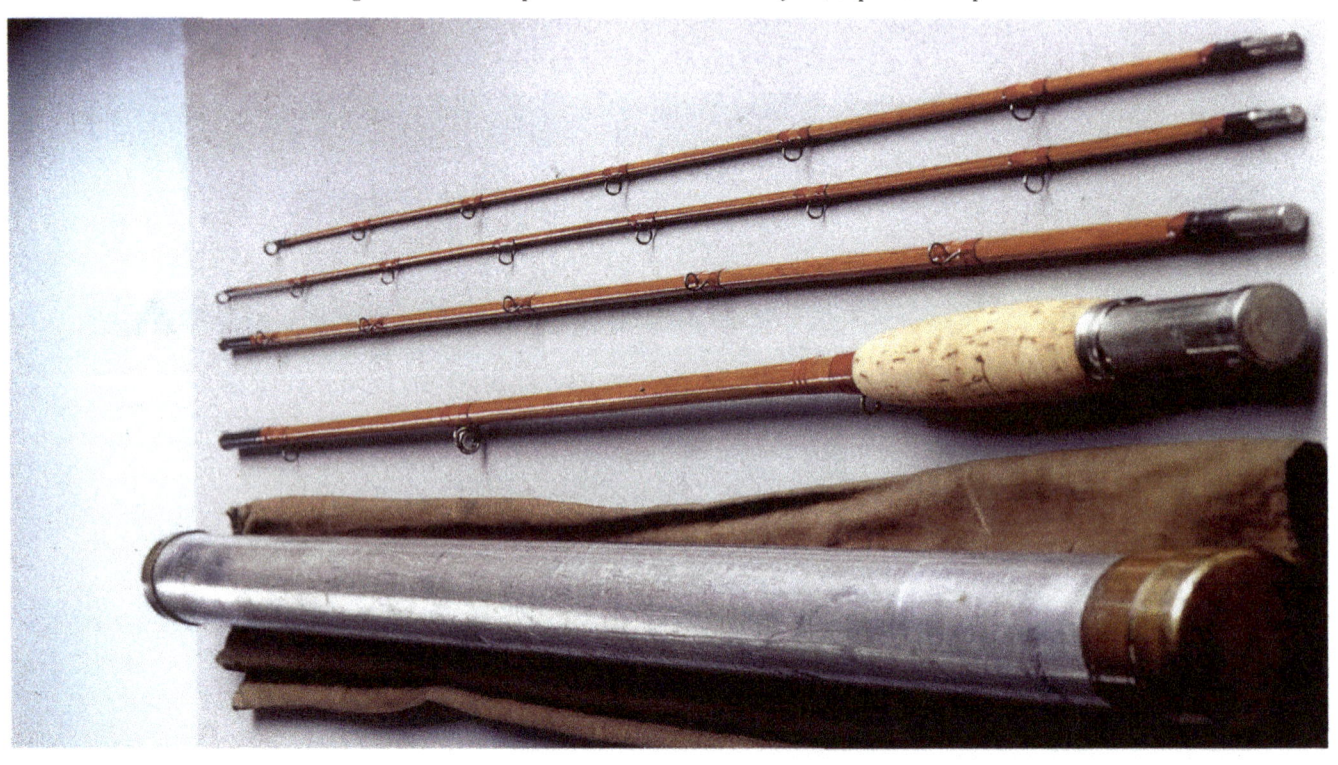

74 ❦ CANE RODS: TIPS & TAPERS

Taper Collection: Leonard

Maker	Leonard	Leonard	Leonard	Leonard	Leonard	Leonard
Model	804	4099 1/2		Tournament	Special Tournament	Duracane
Length	8'-0" x 2pc	8'-6" x 3pc	6'-10"	9'-6" x 3pc	9'-0" x 3pc	8'-0" x 2pc
Line Size	4wt	8/9wt	4/5wt			
Station "d"	"d"	"d"	"d"	"d"	"d"	"d"
0	0.075	0.075	0.068	0.07	0.066	0.074
5	0.09	0.097	0.091	0.085	0.083	0.084
10	0.1	0.111	0.108	0.105	0.1	0.101
15	0.11	0.13	0.124	0.127	0.115	0.114
20	0.126	0.145	0.141	0.145	0.13	0.13
25	0.138	0.153	0.151	0.16	0.149	0.144
30	0.16	0.167	0.155	0.172	0.159	0.157
35	0.167	0.188	0.169	0.187	0.175	0.171
40	0.18	0.195	0.192	0.203	0.184	0.189
45	0.19	0.212	0.203	0.225	0.197	0.202
50	0.199	0.23	0.212	0.236	0.213	0.216
55	0.219	0.245	0.217	0.252	0.225	0.232
60	0.228	0.257	0.221	0.268	0.237	0.242
65	0.249	0.272	0.241	0.28	0.248	0.255
70	0.264	0.292	0.314	0.287	0.255	0.266
75	0.283	0.308	0.349	0.298	0.265	0.285
80	0.294	0.322	0.36	0.315	0.284	0.294
85	0.308	swell 0.337		0.335	0.309	0.31
90	0.32	swell 0.358		0.35	0.332	handle
95	0.333	swell 0.402		0.367	0.351	handle
100		handle		0.385	station 96 = 0.355	
105		handle		handle	station 97 = 0.367	
110				handle	station 98 = 0.390	
					station 99 = 0.455	

Fig. 86: Eight-foot, 3-piece Leonard Model 39.

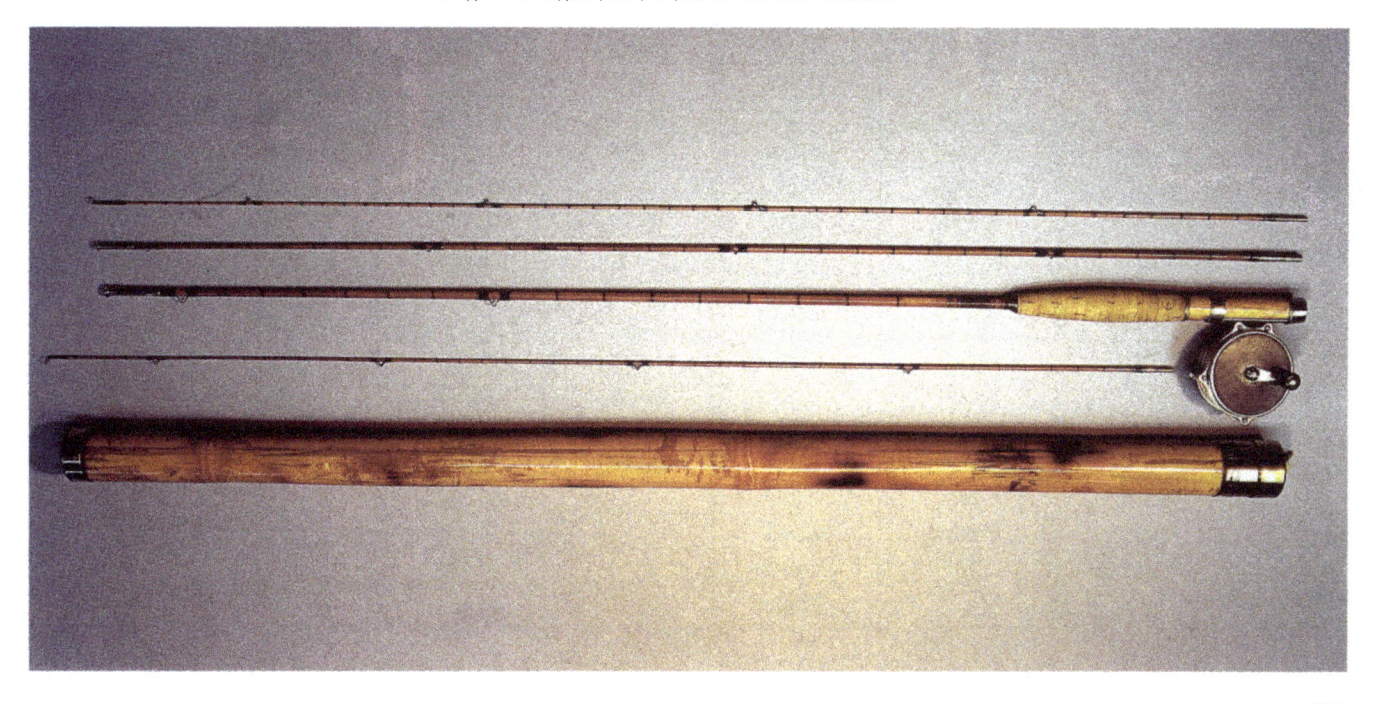

Taper Collection: Lohkamp, McClane, Nunley, Orvis

Maker	Lohkamp	McClane	Nunley	Nunley	Nunley	Orvis	Orvis
Model		Pentagonal	Mt. Creek	1 piece		5/9 Ultralite	Flea
Length	7'-6"	8'-0"	5'-6"	5'-0"	8'-0"	5'-9"	6'-0"
Line Size	5wt	by Faggeter	4wt	2wt	5wt	3/4wt	
Station		center to flat					
"d"	"d"	"d"	"d"	"d"	"d"	"d"	"d"
0	0.066	0.034	0.066	0.06	0.067	0.075	0.078
5	0.074	0.042	0.072	0.064	0.071	0.092	0.093
10	0.088	0.05	0.094	0.085	0.09	0.105	0.105
15	0.103	0.06	0.108	0.097	0.107	0.117	0.117
20	0.118	0.067	0.126	0.113	0.12	0.13	0.128
25	0.133	0.073	0.14	0.126	0.14	0.135	0.14
30	0.149	0.08	0.156	0.142	0.153	0.14	0.153
35	0.165	0.088	0.166	0.151	0.17	0.15	0.155
40	0.181	0.095	0.176	0.161	0.188	0.162	0.166
45	0.198	0.103	0.19	0.173	0.203	0.188	0.185
50	0.215	0.109	0.224	0.231	0.216	0.203	0.196
55	0.231	0.116	0.24	0.235	0.225	0.224	0.205
60	0.248	0.123	0.25	0.235	0.233	0.245	0.217
65	0.265	0.132	0.25		0.242	0.245	0.234
70	0.281	0.14	66 0.25		0.251	0.245	0.263
75	0.298	0.147			0.259		
80	0.314	0.156			0.272		
85	0.331	0.161			0.289		
90	0.347	0.161			0.289		
95		0.161			0.289a		

Taper Collection: Orvis

Maker	Orvis	Orvis	Orvis	Orvis	Orvis	Orvis	Orvis
Model	663	Superfine	Battenkill	Mitey Mite	Battenkill	Mitey Mite	Superfine
Length	6'-6" x3pc	6'-6" x 2pc	7/4 x 3pc	5'-0" x 2pc	6'-6" 2pc	5'-0" x 2pc	6'-0" x 1pc
Line Size	5wt	5/6wt	3wt		5/6wt		5wt
Station							
"d"	"d"	"d"	"d"	"d"	"d"	"d"	"d"
0	0.058	0.076	0.058	0.078	0.075	0.084	0.074
5	0.072	0.094	0.075	0.089	0.094	0.096	0.092
10	0.08	0.111	0.093	0.1	0.111	0.105	0.112
15	0.092	0.124	0.111	0.108	0.122	0.125	0.122
20	0.118	0.133	0.124	0.123	0.133	0.134	0.135
25	0.132	0.144	0.135	0.14	0.141	0.146	0.15
30	0.146	0.159	0.143	0.16	0.152	0.162	0.156
35	0.165	0.164	0.16	0.183	0.164	0.168	0.169
40	0.18	0.17	0.168	0.203	0.18	0.184	0.179
45	0.195	0.19	0.175	0.221	0.197	0.203	0.192
50	0.21	0.194	0.187	0.243	0.209	0.228	0.204
55	0.23	0.207	0.205	Handle	0.218	0.246	0.221
60	0.245	0.226	0.222	Handle	0.23	0.262	0.24
65	0.27	0.231	0.228	Handle	0.245		0.268
70	0.285	0.246	0.248		0.262		
75	0.29	0.261	Handle		0.277		
80	78 0.300	0.261	Handle		0.292		
85			handle				

76 ● Cane Rods: Tips & Tapers

Taper Collection: Orvis

Maker	Orvis	Orvis	Orvis	Orvis	Orvis	Orvis	Orvis
Model	7/3	Midge	Battenkill	Wes Jordon	Battenkill	Battenkill	Limestone
Length	7'-0"	7'-6"	7'-6"	7'-6" x2pc	8'-0" x2pc	8'-0" x2pc	8'-6" x 2pc
Line Size				6wt	7wt	8wt	8wt
Station	"d"	"d"	"d"	"d"	"d"	"d"	"d"
0	0.065	0.075	0.082	0.085	0.08	0.084	0.075
5	0.086	0.095	0.099	0.1	0.095	0.116	0.093
10	0.102	0.108	0.116	0.117	0.117	0.128	0.111
15	0.112	0.121	0.129	0.13	0.132	0.146	0.121
20	0.125	0.132	0.141	0.144	0.144	0.158	0.132
25	0.132	0.142	0.153	0.153	0.156	0.167	0.151
30	0.132	0.154	0.161	0.16	0.168	0.18	0.156
35	0.138	0.161	0.174	0.167	0.18	0.185	0.179
40	0.146	0.168	0.188	0.177	0.192	0.193	0.187
45	0.156	0.189	0.197	0.194	0.204	0.201	0.197
50	0.18	0.2	0.22	0.216	0.215	0.221	0.211
55	0.198	0.221	0.235	0.228	0.228	0.232	0.225
60	0.215	0.235	0.249	0.24	0.241	0.233	0.233
65	0.232	0.247	0.27	0.256	0.254	0.252	0.24
70	0.25	0.26	0.282	0.273	0.268	0.262	0.25
75	0.265	0.28	0.293	0.28	0.284	0.281	0.263
80	0.283	0.295	0.306	0.319	0.303	0.296	0.277
85	0.292	0.31	0.319	0.319	0.33	0.328	0.3
90		0.325	0.333	0.319	0.33	handle	0.324
95					0.33	handle	handle

Fig. 88: Orvis Battenkill 8-foot, 2-piece.

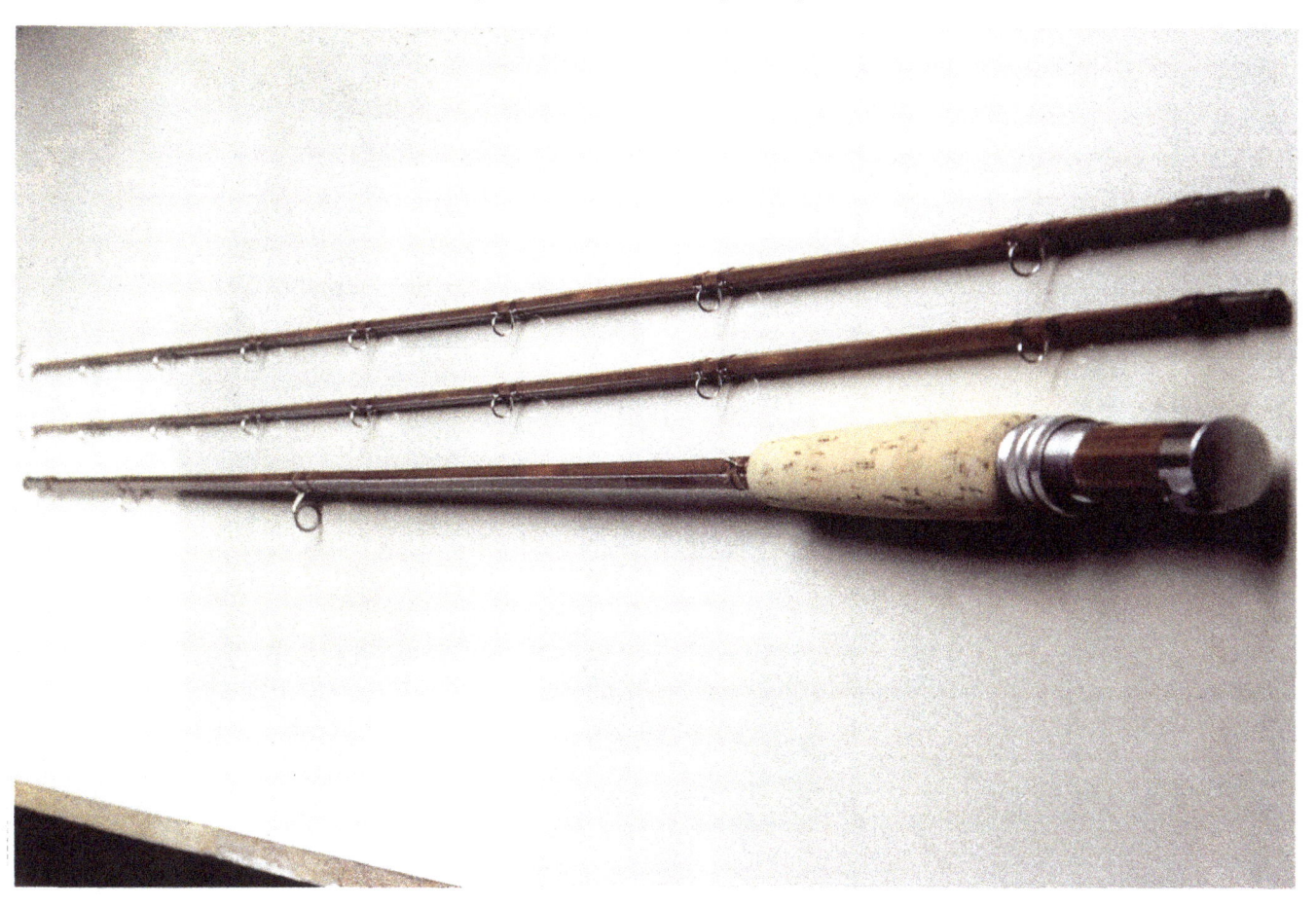

Taper Collection: Orvis, Payne

Maker	Orvis	Payne	Payne	J.Payne	J.Payne	Payne	Payne
Model	Superlight			96	97	98	100
Length	6'-6" x 2pc	4'-4" x 1pc	8'-0" x 2pc	6'-6" x 2pc	7'-0" x 2pc	7'-0" x 2pc	7'-6" x 2pc
Line Size	Spinning Rod	4wt		4wt	4wt	4wt	4wt
Station	"d"	"d"	"d"	"d"	"d"	"d"	"d"
0	0.087	0.076	0.065	0.057	0.064	0.066	0.064
5	0.1	0.092	0.077	0.074	0.076	0.082	0.07
10	0.117	0.118	0.098	0.091	0.098	0.092	0.086
15	0.124	0.124	0.117	0.106	0.112	0.11	0.101
20	0.137	0.138	0.129	0.119	0.126	0.122	0.116
25	0.147	0.154	0.144	0.135	0.138	0.137	0.131
30	0.158	0.168	0.161	0.148	0.15	0.147	0.143
35	0.171	0.178	0.178	0.16	0.162	0.159	0.155
40	ferrule	0.188	0.198	0.168	0.174	0.171	0.167
45	0.217	0.202	0.219	0.178	0.186	0.194	0.18
50	0.233	0.202	0.232	0.196	0.19	0.205	0.191
55	0.251	52=0.202	0.241	0.214	0.206	0.22	0.203
60	0.266		0.249	0.232	0.22	0.242	0.218
65	0.286		0.264	0.252	0.232	0.261	0.231
70	handle		0.279	0.294	0.244	0.281	0.244
75	handle		0.3	0.294	0.252	0.312	0.268
80			0.311	78=0.294	0.28	0.316	0.3
85			0.336		0.3		0.3
90							0.3

Taper Collection: Payne

Maker	J. Payne	J. Payne	J. Payne	E.Payne	E. Payne	Payne	J.Payne
Model	101	102	200	204L	400	Para	79 Para
Length	7'-4" x 2pc	8'-0" x 2pc	8'-0" x 3pc	8'-6" x 3pc	9'-0" x 3pc	7'-1" x 2pc	7'-9" x 2pc
Line Size	5wt	5wt	4wt	5wt		4wt	6/7wt
Station	"d"	"d"	"d"	"d"	"d"	"d"	"d"
0	0.063	0.064	0.056	0.065	0.087	0.058	0.074
5	0.095	0.086	0.072	0.072	0.098	0.071	0.108
10	0.108	0.106	0.086	0.084	0.117	0.097	0.13
15	0.123	0.118	0.102	0.094	0.133	0.113	0.149
20	0.136	0.13	0.116	0.109	0.152	0.129	0.164
25	0.157	0.144	0.13	0.129	0.167	0.143	0.175
30	0.165	0.157	0.138	0.142	0.187	0.15	0.191
35	0.175	0.17	0.153	0.157	0.191	0.151	0.198
40	0.187	0.182	0.17	0.175	0.219	0.155	0.204
45	0.213	0.194	0.188	0.189	0.236	0.155	0.207
50	0.226	0.206	0.198	0.205	0.25	0.182	0.229
55	0.242	0.225	0.209	0.218	0.261	0.198	0.245
60	0.258	0.236	0.218	0.232	0.275	0.21	0.253
65	0.28	0.25	0.223	0.247	0.281	0.222	0.272
70	0.301	0.27	0.239	0.262	0.292	0.244	0.281
75	0.33	0.284	0.254	0.276	0.308	0.26	0.304
80		0.306	0.271	0.287	0.327	0.283	0.345
85		0.328	0.332	0.297	0.341		
90			86=0.344	0.309	0.356		
95			handle	0.32	0.404		
100			handle	0.33	0.45		
105				0.335	0.46		
110					0.46		

Taper Collection: Pezon & Michel, Philipson

Maker	Pezon & Michel	Pezon & Michel	Pezon & Michel	Pezon & Michel	Phillipson	Phillipson
Model	Super parabolic	Colorado	Creusevant	Luxor Classic	Pacemaker	Premium
Length	7'-7" x 2pc	7'-7" x 2pc	8'-3" x 2pc	7'-3" x 2pc	8'-0" x 3pc	9'-0" x 3pc
Line Size	5/6wt	5wt		Spinning Rod	5wt	8wt
Station	"d"	"d"	"d"	"d"	"d"	"d"
0	0.082	0.079	0.086	0.116	0.065	0.076
5	0.095	0.094	0.099	0.125	0.077	0.089
10	0.12	0.11	0.117	0.14	0.088	0.11
15	0.132	0.13	0.133	0.157	0.101	0.125
20	0.145	0.146	0.144	0.177	0.117	0.143
25	0.16	0.161	0.156	0.195	0.129	0.156
30	0.176	0.173	0.171	0.216	0.141	0.169
35	0.189	0.185	0.187	0.226	0.172	0.171
40	0.205	0.201	0.204	0.247	0.184	0.199
45	0.214	0.22	0.217	0.263	0.196	0.226
50	0.232	0.228	0.23	0.28	0.206	0.239
55	0.238	0.232	0.257	0.295	0.215	0.248
60	0.245	0.24	0.271	0.307	0.22	0.258
65	0.252	0.252	0.279	0.323	0.254	0.254
70	0.259	0.256	0.287	handle	0.272	0.257
75	0.264	0.264	0.256	handle	0.284	0.28
80	0.267	0.268	0.3		0.294	0.303
85	0.269	0.272	0.308		82 0.298	0.324
90	Handle		0.313		swell	0.335
95						0.351
100						97 0.389

Taper Collection: Phillipson, Powell

Maker	Phillipson	Phillipson	Phillipson	Phillipson	Powell	Powell	Powell
Model	Smuggler	Peerless	Ed M. Hunter	Powerpak			hollow
Length	7'-8" x 4pc	7'-0" x 2pc	8 1/2 ft x 3pc	8'-6" x 3pc	5'-0" x 2pc	7'-6" x 2pc	9'-6" x 2pc
Line Size	6/7wt	5wt		5wt	5wt	6wt	7wt tip
Station							
	"d"	"d"	"d"	"d"	"d"	"d"	"d"
0	0.083	0.062	0.075	0.077	0.075	0.074	0.081
5	0.099	0.078	0.091	0.099	0.079	0.083	0.099
10	0.119	0.097	0.106	0.112	0.095	0.1	0.113
15	0.133	0.116	0.118	0.135	0.116	0.112	0.126
20	0.155	0.13	0.123	0.151	0.134	0.126	0.146
25	0.176	0.142	0.156	0.154	0.136	0.142	0.167
30	0.181	0.156	0.169	0.16	0.15	0.159	0.18
35	0.19	0.172	0.179	0.177	0.176	0.172	0.193
40	0.207	0.186	0.201	0.195	0.188	0.187	0.216
45	0.221	0.227	0.211	0.212	0.2	0.202	0.233
50	0.235	0.248	0.23	0.226	0.226	0.207	0.252
55	0.252	0.265	0.232	0.242	handle	0.222	0.269
60	0.268	0.272	0.239	0.241		0.239	0.274
65	0.283	0.285	0.243	0.243		0.245	0.29
70	0.301	0.313	0.273	0.269		0.267	0.31
75	0.294		0.285	0.289		0.299	0.317
80	0.336		0.307	0.299		0.311	0.331
85	handle		0.318	0.314		handle	0.355
90			0.322	0.339			0.374
95			handle	0.375			0.38
100			handle	0.375			0.392
105				0.375			0.408
110							0.438

Taper Collection: South Bend, Thomas

Maker	South Bend	Thomas, F.E.	Thomas, F.E.	Thomas, F.E.	Thomas, F.E.	Thomas, F.E.
Model	634-5	Special	Streamer	Special		Dirigo
Length	5'-0" x 1pc	8'-0" x 3pc	9'-0" x 3pc	8'-6" x 3pc	7'-6" x 3pc	9'-0" x 3pc
Line Size	Bait Caster	4wt		5wt	4wt	6wt
Station						
	"d"	"d"	"d"	"d"	"d"	"d"
0	0.106	0.062	0.078	0.06	0.08	0.059
5	0.116	0.075	0.094	0.079	0.095	0.088
10	0.118	0.103	0.119	0.101	0.117	0.1
15	0.135	0.118	0.14	0.117	0.132	0.133
20	0.142	0.13	0.156	0.145	0.144	0.145
25	0.147	0.142	0.166	0.151	0.156	0.153
30	0.216	0.153	0.176	0.166	0.168	0.169
35	0.22	0.165	0.185	0.166	0.18	0.185
40	0.243	0.183	0.193	0.18	0.192	0.195
45	0.308	0.192	0.211	0.193	0.204	0.215
50	0.351	0.204	0.23	0.218	0.215	0.231
55	Handle	0.216	0.245	0.239	0.228	0.245
60		0.228	0.255	0.248	0.241	0.247
65		0.234	0.267	0.246	0.254	0.259
70		0.258	0.28	0.26	0.268	0.27
75		0.274	0.292	0.27	0.284	0.29
80		0.285	0.304	0.289	0.303	0.312
85		0.304	0.321	0.3	0.33	0.325
90		87 = 0.314	0.344	0.357	0.33	0.339
95		handle	0.422	92 = 0.400		96 = 0.385
100			96 = 0.437	handle		handle
105			handle			handle

Fig. 89: South Bend #59, 9-foot, 3-piece x 2 tip.

Taper Collection: Thomas, Thramer, Uslan, Waara, Winston

Maker	Thomas & Thomas	Thomas &Thomas	Thramer	Uslan	Waara	Winston
Model	One Piece	Caenis	444DX	Spencer 9016		#7057
Length	6'-0"	7'-6" x 2pc	4'-4"	Pentagonal	7'-6"	9ft x 2pc
Line Size		3 wt	4wt	9'-0" x 2pc	5wt	7wt
Station						
	"d"	"d"	"d"	flat to center	"d"	"d"
0	0.064	0.058	0.068	0.044	0.072	0.071
5	0.075	0.07	0.084	0.051	0.092	0.094
10	0.088	0.088	0.096	0.057	0.108	0.12
15	0.103	0.108	0.114	0.066	0.124	0.129
20	0.127	0.123	0.128	0.076	0.14	0.147
25	0.14	0.141	0.144	0.085	0.158	0.167
30	0.15	0.155	0.158	0.095	0.17	0.176
35	0.16	0.171	0.176	0.103	0.184	0.19
40	0.172	0.185	0.192	0.107	0.196	0.206
45	0.187	0.195	0.22	0.115	0.21	0.226
50	0.195	0.2	0.248	0.12	0.22	0.238
55	0.213	0.214	0.25	0.123	0.23	0.255
60		0.23		0.125	0.24	0.277
65		0.239		0.133	0.25	0.293
70		0.254		0.144	0.28	0.301
75		0.265		0.151	0.306	0.305
80		79.5 = 0.279		0.159	0.325	0.327
85		80.5 = 0.36		0.167	0.325	0.35
90		Handle		0.171	0.325	0.368
95				0.171		0.385
100				handle		0.368
105				handle		handle

Taper Collection: Winston, Whitehead, Wright & McGill

Maker	Winston	Winston	Winston	Winston	Winston	Whitehead	Wright & McGill
Model	Hollow				Hollow		Stream & Lake
Length	8'-0" x 2pc	8'-0" x 2pc	8'-0" x 2pc	7'-0" x 2pc	8'-6" x 2pc	7'-6"	9'-6" x 3pc
Line Size	5wt		5wt	4wt		5wt	
Station	"d"	"d"	"d"	"d"	"d"	"d"	"d"
0	0.082	0.07	0.078	0.062	0.08	0.068	0.066
5	0.089	0.09	0.085	0.073	0.1	0.084	0.083
10	0.106	0.108	0.102	0.093	0.116	0.1	0.106
15	0.124	0.127	0.12	0.11	0.13	0.118	0.127
20	0.128	0.145	0.124	0.123	0.153	0.132	0.143
25	0.15	0.167	0.146	0.135	0.166	0.145	0.155
30	0.168	0.175	0.164	0.147	0.183	0.16	0.17
35	0.184	0.196	0.18	0.161	0.203	0.171	0.189
40	0.194	0.21	0.19	0.179	0.22	0.179	0.205
45	0.217	0.217	0.213	0.198	0.23	0.201	0.226
50	0.222	0.225	0.218	0.214	0.245	0.211	0.249
55	0.23	0.237	0.226	0.223	0.26	0.217	0.253
60	0.24	0.245	0.236	0.241	0.27	0.234	0.275
65	0.249	0.25	0.245	0.257	0.283	0.251	0.278
70	0.263	0.263	0.259	0.279	0.293	0.269	0.286
75	0.277	0.282	0.273	0.287	0.303	0.279	0.293
80	0.285	0.292	0.281	handle	0.315	0.306	0.317
85	0.304	0.295	0.3	handle	0.328	0.312	0.331
90	handle	handle	handle		0.34	0.315	0.343
95	handle	handle	handle		0.353		0.358
100					handle		0.371
105					handle		104 = 0.428
110							handle

Taper Collection: Wright & McGill, Young

Maker	Wright & McGill	Young, P.H.	Young, P.H.	Young, P.H.	Young, P.H.	Young, P.H.
Model	Granger Aristocrat	Para 15	Para 15	Texas general	Para 16	
Length	8'-6" x 3pc	8'0" x 2pc	8'-0"	8'-0" x 2pc	8'-6"	9'-0"
Line Size	5wt	6wt	5wt	7/8wt	6/7wt	9wt
Station						
	"d"	"d"	"d"	"d"	"d"	"d"
0	0.086	0.075	0.07	0.087	0.077	0.092
5	0.091	0.089	0.086	0.114	0.087	0.108
10	0.106	0.116	0.107	0.14	0.113	0.13
15	0.114	0.122	0.123	0.16	0.144	0.145
20	0.121	0.14	0.138	0.166	0.178	0.174
25	0.134	0.165	0.157	0.185	0.187	0.192
30	0.161	0.187	0.17	0.201	0.203	0.207
35	0.181	0.193	0.189	0.226	0.209	0.22
40	0.186	0.203	0.208	0.236	0.23	0.244
45	0.196	0.226	0.225	0.24	0.247	0.25
50	0.206	0.231	0.239	0.246	0.259	0.264
55	0.226	0.249	0.252	0.272	0.262	0.265
60	0.231	0.256	0.26	0.289	0.277	0.272
65	0.232	0.267	0.268	0.279	0.292	0.282
70	0.264	0.265	0.277	0.293	0.302	0.302
75	0.284	0.274	0.288	0.311	0.302	0.312
80	0.294	0.294	0.3"	0.312	0.302	0.326
86	0.301	0.286		0.326	0.302	0.338
90	0.344	handle		0.331	0.302	0.36
95	handle	handle		handle	0.302	0.367
100	handle			handle	0.302	0.368
105						0.37
110						0.37

Taper Collection: Young

Maker	Young, P.H.	Young, P.H.	Young, P.H.	Young, P.H.	Young, P.H.	Young, P.H.
Model	McClouth's	Perfectionist	Midge	Para 14	Driggs River	Para 17
Length	8'-3" x 2pc	7'-6"	6'-3"	7'-9"	7'-2"	8'-6" x 2pc
Line Size	7/8wt	4wt	4wt	5wt	5wt	8wt
Station						
	"d"	"d"	"d"	"d"	"d"	"d"
0	0.075	0.07	0.063	0.072	0.07	0.085
5	0.095	0.081	0.073	0.088	0.09	0.098
10	0.12	0.094	0.092	0.1	0.108	0.113
15	0.135	0.115	0.108	0.117	0.127	0.131
20	0.154	0.134	0.12	0.133	0.142	0.155
25	0.175	0.146	0.136	0.15	0.152	0.178
30	0.192	0.155	0.146	0.167	0.16	0.194
35	0.205	0.17	0.166	0.183	0.185	0.209
40	0.209	0.192	0.179	0.2	0.199	0.218
45	0.223	0.203	0.198	0.21	0.209	0.232
50	0.241	0.214	0.202	0.221	0.218	0.248
55	0.259	0.225	0.218	0.231	0.229	0.262
60	0.27	0.238	0.226	0.24	0.25	0.264
65	0.283	0.247	0.236	0.248	0.258	0.27
70	0.303	0.258	handle	0.257	0.263	0.282
75	0.319	0.268	handle	0.265	0.265	0.294
80	0.33	0.275		0.273	0.267	0.305
85	0.346	0.275		0.285	0.269	0.313
90	handle	0.275		handle	0.269	0.322
95	handle			handle		0.322
100						0.322
105						0.322

Taper Collection: Young, Gould

Maker	Young, P.H.	Young, P.H.	Young, P.H.	Young, P.H.	Gould	Gould	Gould
Model	Spinmaster	Special	Spincaster	Steelhead	RR166	RR171	RR170
Length	7'-2" x 2pc	6'-4" x 2pc	6'-3" x 2pc	8'-9" x 2pc	7'-10"	8'-0"	8'-0"
Line size	Spinning Rod	Spinning rod	Spinning Rod	Spinning Rod	6 wt.	5 wt.	7 wt
Station "d"	"d"	"d"	"d"	"d"	"d"	"d"	"d"
0	0.082	0.098	0.096	0.132	0.075	0.073	0.075
5	0.091	0.101	0.098	0.14	0.100	0.092	0.100
10	0.106	0.122	0.115	0.158	0.122	0.115	0.122
15	0.126	0.148	0.142	0.188	0.146	0.138	0.146
20	0.143	0.158	0.158	0.214	0.165	0.152	0.165
25	0.157	0.17	0.174	0.232	0.179	0.167	0.179
30	0.176	0.194	0.191	0.245	0.194	0.179	0.194
35	0.192	0.224	0.219	0.26	0.205	0.194	0.205
40	0.207	0.226	0.216	0.268	0.214	0.206	0.214
45	0.208	0.238	0.224	0.276	0.221	0.215	0.221
50	0.211	0.24	0.241	0.298	0.235	0.224	0.230
55	0.216	0.257	0.25		0.247	0.227	0.245
60	0.226	0.268	0.266	0.325	0.258	0.238	0.262
65	0.246	0.285	0.274	0.336	0.275	0.256	0.278
70	0.255			0.342	0.292	0.273	0.292
75	0.259			0.363	0.305	0.290	0.305
80				0.38	0.326	0.312	0.326
85				0.403	0.339	0.324	0.339
90					0.346	0.349	0.346
95					0.350	0.350	0.350

Fig. 90: Chamberlain's custom fly-tying case.

Best-of-the-Best Gould Tapers

It's always difficult for a new rod builder to figure out which rod to build. What follows is a recommended selection of eleven of my tapers covering a wide variety of uses. The tapers are medium, fast, or extra-fast actions, and include a short rod, a hollow rod, ordinary trout rods, rods with a "swell in the butt", graphite insert rods, and a taper suitable for steelhead and salmon. All of these can be built without extra-special machinery. The taper information is listed in the taper collection including the line size. Note that this recommended list covers line weights from 4-8. Three of these (RR-84-8, RR-95-8 1/4GI, and RR-117-8 1/2GI) are models that the author uses extensively in his fishing in British Columbia and Alaska.

Model	Rise	Line Wt.	Sections	Comments
RR-134-6	0.314 xfast	5	2	Light weight with surprising power; completely finished rod weighs 3 1/2 oz.
RR-108-7	0.274 medium	4	2	A personal favorite; completely finished rod weighs 3 1/2 oz.
RR-135-7	0.316 xfast	4	2	Has very mild swell in the butt
RR-51-7 1/2	0.276 medium	5/6	2	One of those rods that just turn out beautifully - named "The Dutchess"
RR-139H - 7 1/2	0.288 fast	5	2	Hollow built with pleasant action; completely finished rod weighs 4 oz.
RR-84-8	0.286 fast	6/7	2	Excellent all-around trout rod, has swell in the butt feature
RR-151-8	0.290 fast	5	3	Made specially for Joan Wulff, has trip design to prevent hinge effect
RR-95-81/4 GI	0.288 fast	7	2	18" graphite insert, excellent for sink tip, has mild swell in butt.
RR-111-8 1/2	0.286 fast	6/7	2	Similar to Holbrook 308 taper, but has swell in butt feature added.
RR-143-8 1/2GI	0.280 fast	5	3	14" graphite insert, fast tip action
RR-117-8 1/2 GI	0.286 fast	7/8	2	52" graphite insert, excellent for steelhead and salmon, fighting butt.
RR-166-7'-10"	0.272 medium	6	2	Double Parabolic, lots of power
RR-169-8	.280 fast	6/7	2	Double Parabolic
RR-170-9	.280 fast	7	3	Double Parabolic; lovely to cast
RR-171-8	.246 slow	5	3	Double Parabolic

Tip No. 21
Understanding Rod Actions

If there ever was an area of rod building that was difficult to define and put standards around it is the topic of rod actions. Some of the terms encountered are: fast action, slow action, fast tip, parabolic, progressive, straight line, balanced, synchronized, semi-parabolic, swell in the butt, and rise. Most of these actually refer to the taper of the rod which is the design factor controlling the "action" as to how the rod will "feel" when the fly-fisher is casting with it. No matter how closely we try to define the terms, the result is still a subjective matter. Each person has his or her personal preferences.

Common Understandings
To establish some common ground on which to make comparisons it is best to use a visual picture of rod tapers. An excellent way to do this is by utilizing a graph of the taper of a rod where the rod thickness is plotted along the vertical axis and the distance from the tip in 5" increments is plotted along the horizontal axis with the tip on the left and the butt on the right. This is the most common system and has been used for some time now. It has become the standard way of viewing tapers. Familiarization with this layout will allow the cane rod enthusiast to recognize features that contribute to a particular rod action. See Fig. 92.

Definitions
The following glossary defines the terms associated with the taper of a rod and with rod action:

Straight Line Taper: The taper produced as a result of using straight line stresses. That is, when stresses are plotted against position along the rod the line is a straight one, the slope of the line is constant. The plot of rod thickness against position along the rod is also essentially a straight line with constant slope.

Rise: The change in thickness of the rod per 100" of length. It is the slope of the line (taper) when thickness is plotted against distance from the tip. This is calculated using the reasonably straight middle section of the taper from station 10 to station 60 and then extrapolated for 100" so that special effects such

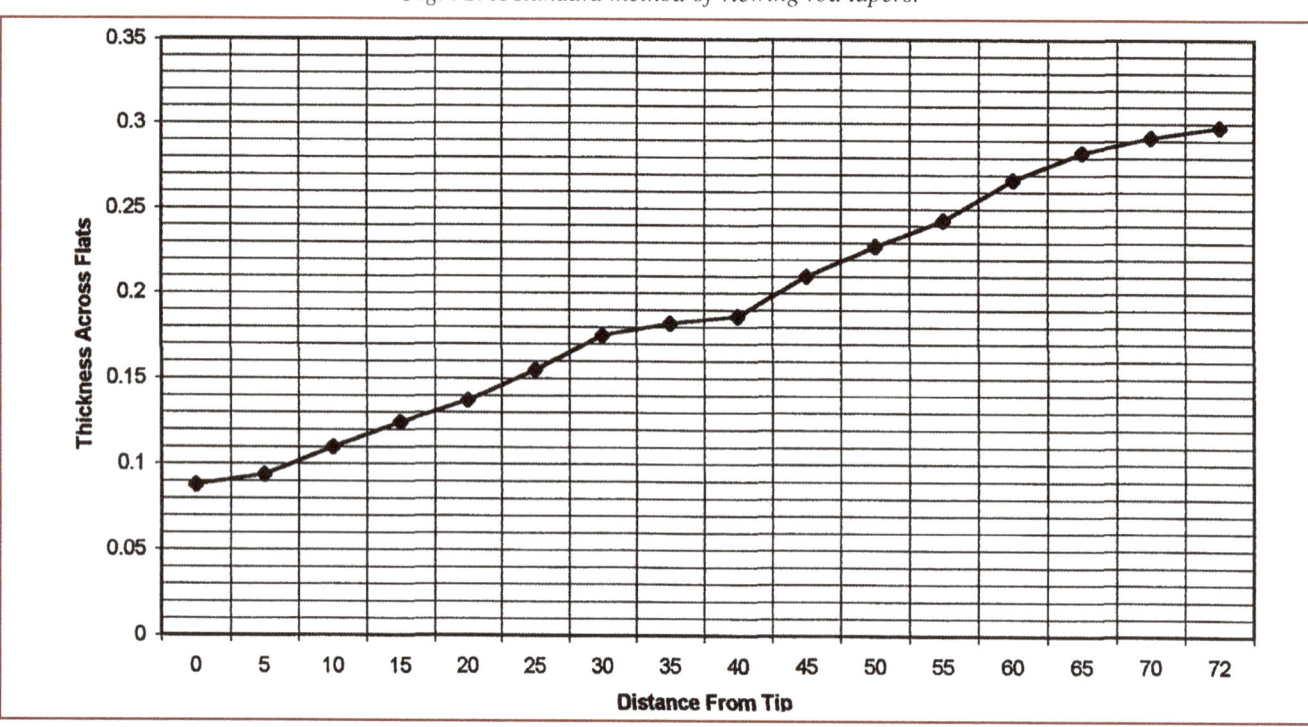

Fig. 92: A standard method of viewing rod tapers.

as "a swell in the butt" and tip stiffening are omitted.

Parabolic: The taper produced when the stresses used form a parabolic curve when stresses are plotted against the position along the rod.

Semi-parabolic: A taper that is between that of a true parabolic and a straight-line taper. The plot of stresses versus position along the rod is a curve lying between the parabolic and the straight line.

Fast Action: A taper that has a steep "rise", the thickness increases relatively fast. This refers to the slope of the line when thickness is plotted against distance from the tip.

Slow Action: A taper that has relatively slower increase in the "rise". Produces what is also called a "soft" action wherein the whole rod flexes substantially.

Fast Tip: A taper design where the tip section is strong enough to prevent too much flexing.

Swell in the Butt: A taper design where the taper is increased dramatically for a short area just in front of the cork grip. Usually, but not always, obvious to the naked eye.

Wave Linear Action: Occurs as the rod transmits energy to the fly line along the length of the rod in the form of a sine wave on the power stroke.

Rise in inches per 100 inches of length	Rod Action
Up to 0.239"	Extra slow
0.240" - 0.260"	Slow
o.261 - 0.280	Medium
0.281 - 0.300	Fast
0.301 and up	Extra fast

Fig. 93: Rise ranges for various rod actions.

Progressive: A taper designed so that the rod produces a wave linear action, generally uniform (or straight line) in taper, but flattens a bit at the ferrule (to offset the stiffness added by the ferrule) and decreases near the tip.

Synchronized: The process of finding the "spine" of each section and locating the guides on the soft side of each section.

Balanced: Placing the center of the hand grasp half way between the balance point and the centerline of the reel.

Rise
The table shown in Fig. 93 depicts what the "rise" ranges should be for tapers with a extra-slow, slow, medium or fast taper.

A pictorial of the data shown above for utilizing the upper limit of each range is shown in the rod action graph in Fig. 94.

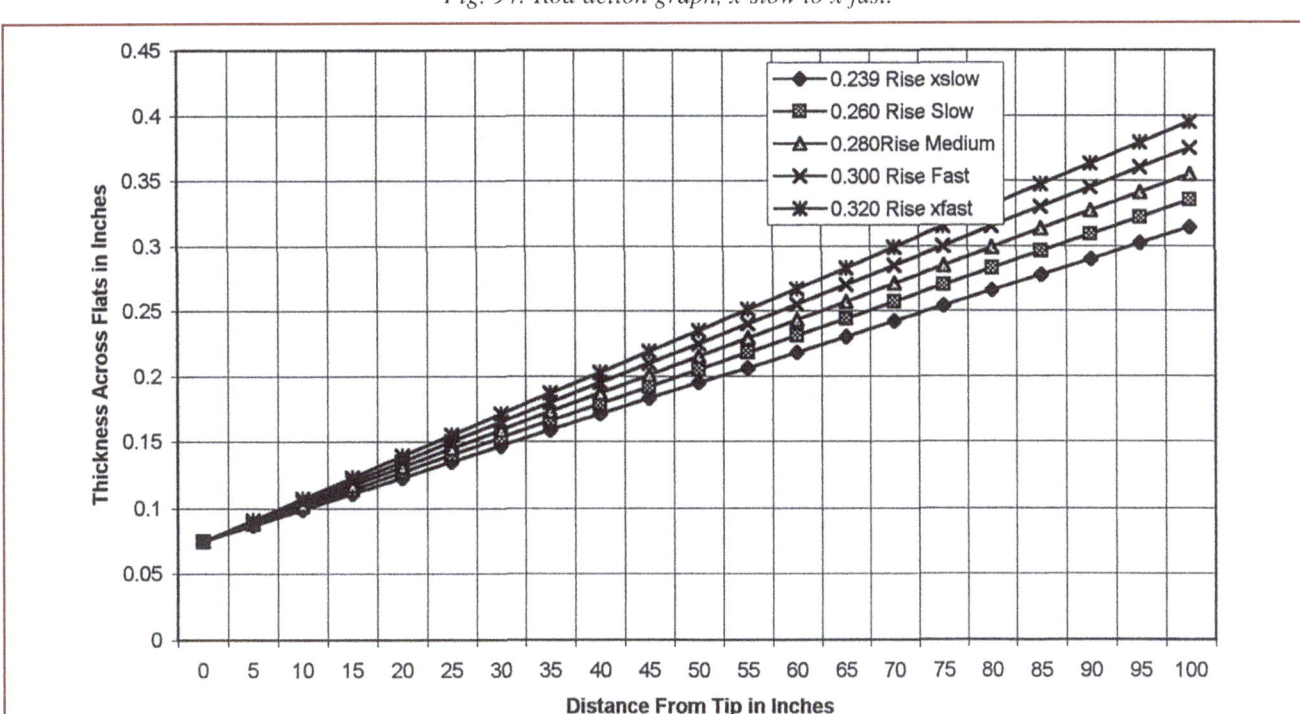

Fig. 94: Rod action graph, x-slow to x-fast.

TIP NO. 21: UNDERSTANDING ROD ACTIONS

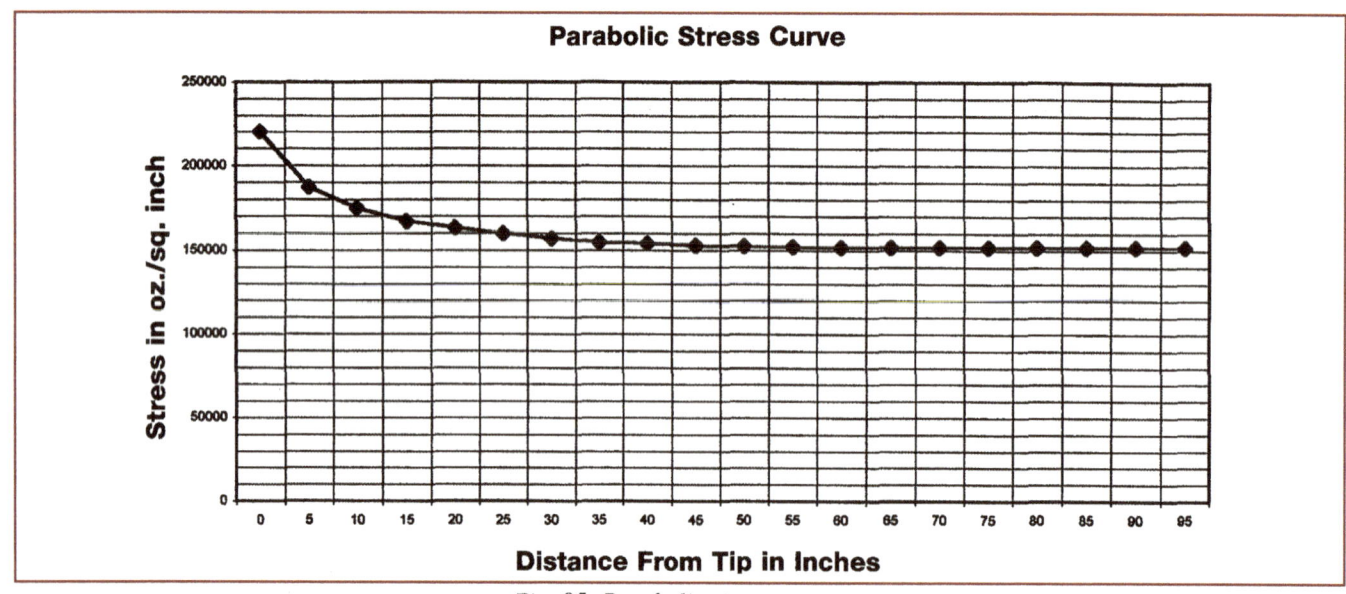

Fig. 95: Parabolic stress curve.

Parabolics

One of the most commonly discussed types of rod tapers is the "parabolic". Let it be stressed again here that a parabolic is defined as a rod whose stress curve is parabolic in nature, not the curve of thickness versus position along the rod. See Fig. 95.

Figure 96 shows the taper produced by this type of stress curve compared to the taper from straight-line stresses when plotted as thickness versus distance from the tip.

Several features stand out in the comparison. One is that the parabolic taper is thicker in the tip section and thinner in the butt section. This means that the whole rod will flex more in the handle and butt section area. Another feature is that the lines intersect at the "80" station which is located just in front of the hand grasp which tends to magnify the whole rod action of the parabolic. To further understand rods with a parabolic-type action, the examination of a Paul Young Driggs River,

Fig. 96: Taper of parabolic compared to straight line.

90 ● CANE RODS: TIPS & TAPERS

favored by many, is in order. A graph of this taper is shown in Fig. 97.

Note the rapid decrease in the taper as it nears the butt end. There is little gain in thickness from station 60 all the way to the butt end of the rod at station 86. The "low" spot in the taper at station 30 is either an anomaly or more likely it is designed into the taper to prevent the tip section from feeling "hinged".

Double Parabolic

Pay special attenton to the rod tapers which are shown as the last three columns on page 86. These rods cast extremely well and are much easier to build than a rod with a major "swell in the butt". The term "double parabolic" is one I've coined to describe a taper which has a parabolic tip section, then is flattenned a bit to offset the ferrule effect and finally has a parabolic butt section. For people who like the way light weight graphite rods feel compared to the old "noodle" type cane rods, they'll really like this design. The casting action is one that produces a great deal of power without much effort. The rod really works for you. This is my favorite and preferred by many customers.

Hollowing Effect

Another taper design feature to understand is the effect of hollowing on the stiffness of the taper. One way to arrive at a reasonable conclusion is to calculate the change in the moment of inertia of the cross section. One standard that has been reached empirically by the author is that the wall thickness of a hollowed hex rod should not be less than 0.070" in order to provide adequate glue joint strength at the seams. For many rods this means that hollowing is done primarily in the butt section. The effect on the moment of inertia decreases as the thickness across the flats decreases. Therefore an average "d" for a butt section will be used in the calculation rather than the size at one end of the butt section or the other. As an example, consider a two-piece rod that has a "d" of 0.200" at the ferrule and 0.375 at the butt. The average "d" would be 0.2875". Now the moment of inertia for this rod section hollowed out with a hexagonal hole in the bore where the wall thickness is 0.070" would be $I = 0.060(d_2^4 - d_1^4)$ noting that $d_2 = 0.2875$" and $d_1 = 0.1475$". Therefore $I = 0.060 (.0068 - 0.00047) = 0.00038$ inches^4. The loss due to hollowing is $0.0004 - 0.00038 = 0.00002$. This is equal to $0.00002/0.0004 = .05 = 5\%$. Also there is additional stiffness when solid dams installed in the hollowed section every 2 1/2" to prevent the walls from collapsing under flexure. This probably adds in another 20% to the moment of inertia resulting in an actual loss total of about 4%. To the rod builder this means that a loss in stiffness of about 4% has to be accounted for in designing the taper of a hollow rod. In the case of rods with a graphite insert, as shown on some of the author's tapers, the hollowing loss is thus offset.

Conversion of Hex to Quadrate Tapers

More than a few rod builders have used a conversion factor of 93% when making a quad taper from a hexagonal rod taper.

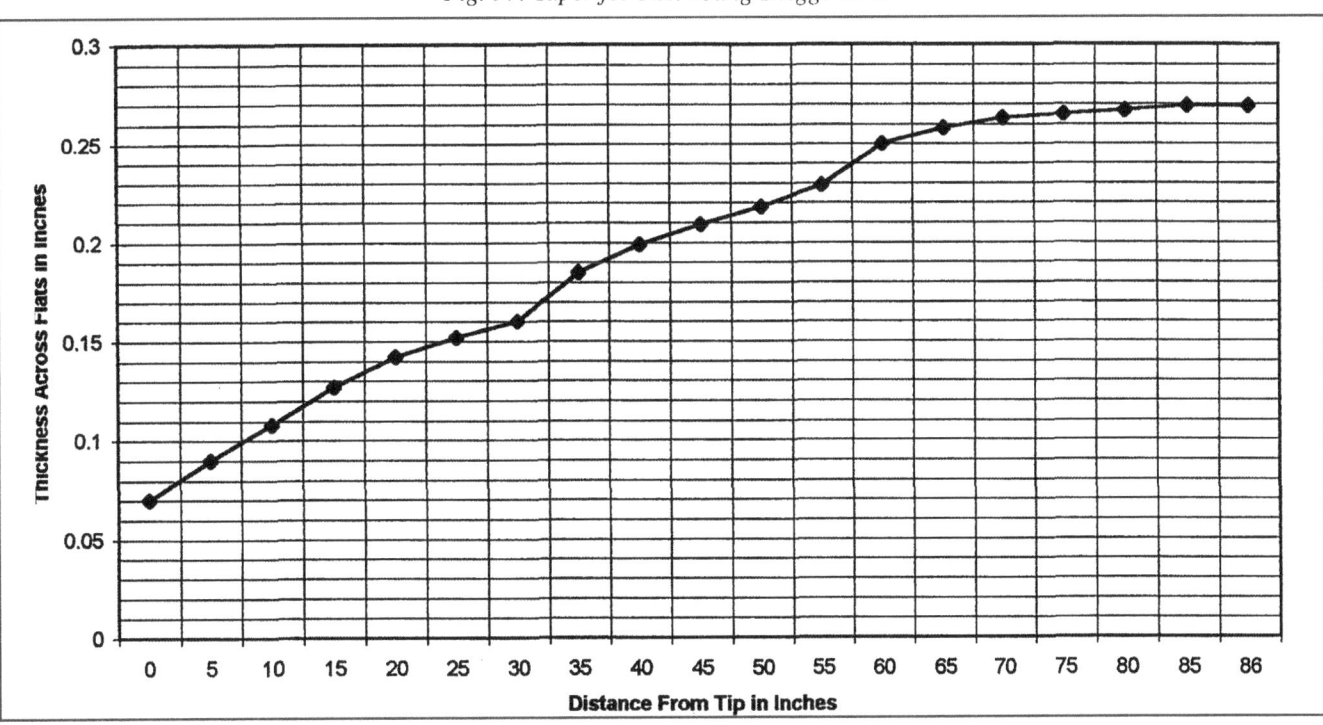

Fig. 97: Taper for P.H. Young Driggs River.

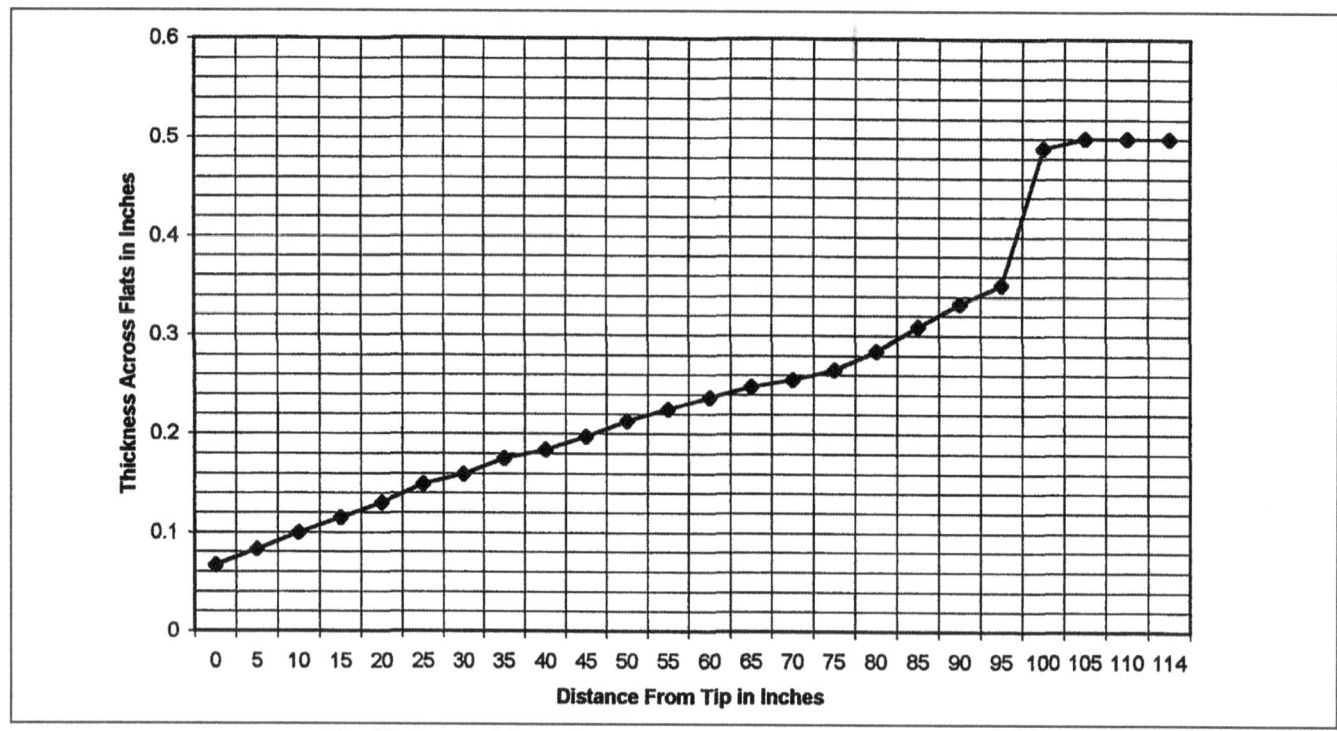

Fig. 98: Leonard Special Tournament taper showing swell in butt.

That is to say since the quad is inherently stiffer than the hex, the hex taper was multiplied by 0.93 to get the corresponding quad taper. The "0.93" factor was determined by assuming equal cross sectional areas. The area of a square = $2d_s^2$ and the area of a hexagon = $0.866d_h^2$, therefore $d_s = 0.93d_h$. The result of using this factor is a quad rod action that is much softer (although it performs somewhat better when fully loaded) than the corresponding hex rod action, disappointing many builders.

A better conversion factor to use is 96.4%. This factor is derived by comparing the moment of inertias "I", an engineering factor indicating stiffness, for the two cross sections. The moment of inertia for a square $I_s = 0.083d^4$. The moment of inertia for a hexagon $I_h = 0.060d^4$. Now for sections of equal areas, let's say $1.000 inches^2$, $I_s = 0.083$ and $I_h = 0.080$. So the conversion factor would be $0.080/0.083 = 0.964$ or 96.4%. When this factor is used in converting the hex taper to a quad instead of the 0.93 factor an increase in the rod thickness of 3.4% will be realized and the rod action of the quad will be more like the hex.

Swell in the Butt

This taper design feature does just what it says, it places a very fast increase in the taper in the butt section located just in front of the cork grip. Depending on how severe the increase is, a special planing form may be required or an adaptation made to an existing form. This feature has been in use for many years and can readily be seen on some of the old masters' rods, such as Leonard's. A swell in the butt is usually but not always obvious to the naked eye. The effect of this taper adjunct is to move the action of the rod away from the handle and down towards the tip but mainly right in front of the grip. This is preferred by many who do not care for the feeling of a rod that flexes in the handle and lean more toward desiring a faster tip action. An example of a taper having a swell in the butt is shown in Fig. 98.

Tip No. 22
Where to Find It

Bamboo
C.H. Demarest Co.
P.O. Box 238
Bloomingdale, N.J. 07403
(973) 492-1414
demaralon@aol.com

Tuxedo Custom Rods
P.O. Box 1167
Stockton, CA 95201
(209) 948-6508

Bluing
Payne's Original Formula
Nickel Silver Oxidizer
The Fly Rod and Room
P.O. Box 565
100 Bonta Lane
Elbridge, NY 13060-0565

Bluing Protective Coating
Aero Gloss Hot Fuel Proof No.65-1
Clear Gloss
From local hobby shop

Computer Taper Design Programs
John Bokstrom
21563 Stonehouse Ave.
Maple Ridge, B.C. V2X 3Z5
(604) 463-3751
bokstrom2axionet.com

Wayne Cattanach
15315 Apple Ave.
Casnovia, MI 49318
cattanach@wmis.net

Cork
C & D Trading
6451 Lyndale Ave., S.
Richfield, MN 55423
(612) 574-1563

The Angler's Supply House
P.O. Box 1044
Woodland, WA 98674
(360) 225-9445
www.anglersworkshop.com

Dial Indicators & Hole Gauges
(Lufkin or Starrett Tool supplier)
Everett Industrial Supply
2201- Pacific Ave.
Everett, WA 98206
(425) 259-9241

Ferrules
Classic Sporting Enterprises
Box 1909 Fitch Hill Road
Hyde Park, Vermont 05655
(802) 888-7859

Angler's Workshop
P.O. Box 1044
Woodland, WA 98674
(360) 225-9445

Research Engineering Co.
72 Shaker Road
Enfield, CT 06082
(860) 749-3476
www.rec.com

E.J. Hille
The Angler's Supply House
811 S. Market St.
S. Williamsport, PA 17702
1-(800) 326-6612

Ferrules for Quadrate Rods
Tony Larson • Pumpkin10@prodigy.net

Ferrule Notching Tool
Use Dremel Grinder with Dremel #7120
Diamond Disc Point bit
Available through local hardware store

Finger Cots
Local office supply store

Finishes
Local paint and hardware stores
For Pratt and Lambert R10
Polyurethane Varnish
Daly's
3525 Stone
Seattle, WA 98103
(206) 633-4200

Glue
For Bamboo-Spline Gluing
Urac 185
The Nelson Paint Co.
One Nelson drive
Kingsford, MI 49801
(906) 774-5566

For Ferrule Gluing and Gluing Reel Seat to Rod
Urethane Bond (U-Bond)
Easypoxy Industrial Adhesives
5485 Nichols Run, Limestone, NY 14753
easypoxy@juno.com
tel/fax (716) 925-7703

For Gluing Cork Rings Together
Elmer's Carpenter's Glue
Local hardware store

Guides and Hook Keepers
Angler's Workshop
P.O. Box 1044
Woodland, WA 98674
(360) 225-9445

Guides
REC
72 Shaker Road
Enfield, Ct 06082
(860) 749-3476

Cabela's
812-13th Ave.
Sydney, Nebraska 69160
1-800-237-4444

Hardware
Comprehensive hardware supply
Gears, Drills, Taps, Dies, etc.

McMaster-Carr Supply Co.
9630 Norwalk Blvd.
Santa Fe Springs, CA 90670-2932
1-(562)-692-5911
www.mcmaster.com

Hardwick's
4214 Roosevelt Way
Seattle, WA
(206) 632-1203

Planes, Block and Scraping and Plane Blades
Lie-Nielsen Tool Works
Route 1
Warren, Maine 04864
(207) 273-2520

Hardwick's
4214 Roosevelt Way
Seattle, WA
(206) 632-1203

Local Hardware Stores

Planing Forms
J.D. Wagner, Inc
6549 Kingsdale Blvd.
Parma Heights, Ohio 44130-3969
(440) 845- 4415

Corens Rod and Reel
6001 N. Nina
Chicago, IL 60631
(773) 631-5202

Golden Witch
P.O. Box 159
Hopeland, PA 17533
(717) 738-7330
www.goldenwitch.com

For drawings to make your own:
See book: *Secrets of the Bamboo Fly Rod*
Ray Gould, pgs. 41, 45, 46, 50, 64.

Reel Seats
Bellinger Reel Seats
1997-25th St., S.E.
Salem, Oregon 98674
(503) 371-6151

Clemens
444 Schantz Spring Road
Allentown, PA 18104
(610) 395-5119

Cabela's
812-13th Ave.
Sidney, Nebraska 69160
1-800-237-4444

Angler's Workshop
P.O. Box 1044
Woodland, WA 98674
(360) 225-9445

REC
72 Shaker Road
Enfield, CT 06082
(860) 749-3476

Venneri's
21 Chuck Hill Road
Saugerties, NY 12477
(845) 246-5882
rvenneri@ulster.net

Tapered Reamers
For fitting cork bore to rod

Clemens
444 Schantz Spring Road
Allentown, PA 18104
(610) 395-5119

Angler's Workshop
P.O. Box 1044
Woodland, WA 98674
(360) 225-9445

Thread
Rod Wrapping Thread

Angler's Workshop
P.O. Box 1044
Woodland, WA 98674
(360) 225-9445

For Invisible Wrapping Threads
Golden Witch
P.O. Box 159
Hopeland, PA 17533
(717) 738-7330

Winding Checks, Nickel Silver
Angler's Workshop
P.O. Box 1044
Woodland, WA 98674
(360) 225-9445

REC
72 Shaker Road
Enfield, CT 06082
(860) 749-3476

Wire, Nickel Silver
For pinning ferrules
TSI
101 Nickerson
P.O. Box 9266
Seattle, WA 98109
1-800-426-9984

Wrapping Stand
See Tip No.10 in this book.

Angler's Workshop
P.O. Box 1044
Woodland, WA 98674
(360) 225-9445

Ray Gould, a long-time Edmonds, Washington resident, graduated from the University of Washington in 1953 with a Master's Degree in Mechanical Engineering. He worked for Scott Paper Company in Everett, Washington for 25 years in various management positions, and as Facilities Director he directed the engineering and maintenance departments.

Community service has played an important role in Gould's life. He was appointed three times by the Governor as a Community College Trustee, won election twice as an Edmonds City Councilman, and served as a County Planning Commissioner. In addition, he was appointed to the Citizen's Oversight Panel for Sound Transit, chaired the Performance Audit Committee for Sound Transit, was a Rotarian for some 30 years, and serves on the Board of 1000 Friends of Washington. Gould was recently named to the Citizen's Cabinet for Snohomish County Executive Aaron Reardon.

Gould become a fly-fisherman in 1958 when he first visited Glimpse Lake, B.C., now his favorite spot on earth. He has served as President of the Northwest Fly Angler's club in Seattle, taught fly tying, and is currently a member of the Olympic Fly Fishers Club of Edmonds.

Gould has been building and repairing bamboo rods since 1978. He uses his engineering background to design and build the necessary tools and equipment and uses computer programs to design the rod tapers. Gould has presented numerous fly-club programs and exhibited in Washington, Montana, and British Columbia, and co-chaired two West Coast bamboo-rod builders workshops at Corbett Lake, British Columbia. His recent "Double Parabolic" rod taper is becoming a hallmark of his work.

Gould and his wife Susan (former State Senator) reside in Edmonds, Washington. They have three children Kevin, Meridith and Lea Ann.

We hope you enjoyed this title from Echo Point Books & Media

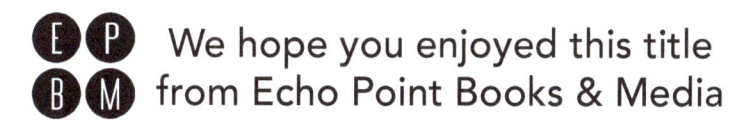

Before Closing this Book, Two Good Things to Know

Buy Direct & Save

Go to www.echopointbooks.com (click "Our Titles" at top or click "For Echo Point Publishing" in the middle) to see our complete list of titles. We publish books on a wide variety of topics—from spirituality to auto repair.

Buy direct and save 10% at www.echopointbooks.com

DISCOUNT CODE: EPBUYER

Make Literary History and Earn $100 Plus Other Goodies Simply for Your Book Recommendation!

At Echo Point Books & Media we specialize in republishing out-of-print books that are united by one essential ingredient: high quality. Do you know of any great books that are no longer actively published? If so, please let us know. If we end up publishing your recommendation, you'll be adding a wee bit to literary culture and a bunch to our publishing efforts.

Here is how we will thank you:

- A free copy of the new version of your beloved book that includes acknowledgement of your skill as a sharp book scout.
- A free copy of another Echo Point title you like from echopointbooks.com.
- And, oh yes, we'll also send you a check for $100.

Since we publish an eclectic list of titles, we're interested in a wide range of books. So please don't be shy if you have obscure tastes or like books with a practical focus. To get a sense of what kind of books we publish, visit us at www.echopointbooks.com.

If you have a book that you think will work for us, send us an email at editorial@echopointbooks.com

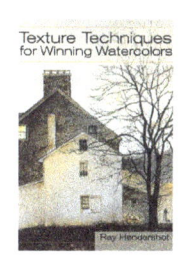

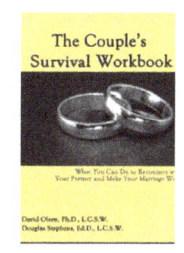

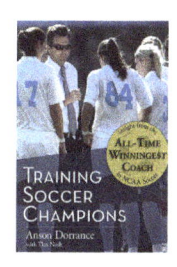

CPSIA information can be obtained
at www.ICGtesting.com
Printed in the USA
LVHW071314250621
691152LV00028B/588